List of Officers

of the

Colonies on the Delaware

and the

Province of Pennsylvania

1614-1776

Edited by

John B. Linn
&
William Henry Egle

Indexed by

Robert Barnes

CLEARFIELD COMPANY

Originally published 1880
Harrisburg, Pennsylvania

Reprinted by
Genealogical Publishing Company, Inc. for
Clearfield Company
1992
Baltimore, Maryland

LIST OF OFFICERS

OF THE

COLONIES ON THE DELAWARE

AND THE

PROVINCE OF PENNSYLVANIA.

1614—1776.

[NOTE.—This List of Officers of the Colony and Province is probably not complete; yet for its preservation, as also reference, we present the imperfect record as it is. The dates are given as we have found them on various commission books. These are those of appointment, assuming of office, or of commission, and in most instances extremely difficult to determine which. As to the orthography, we have been guided mostly by the records, save where the spelling could be otherwise properly authenticated.—*Editors.*]

OFFICERS

OF THE

COLONIES ON THE DELAWARE.

1614—1681.

COLONIES ON THE DELAWARE.

GOVERNORS OF NEW NETHERLANDS AND OF THE DUTCH ON THE DELAWARE.

Capt. Cornelis Jacobsen Mey, } Vice Directors, . . . 1614—1623
Adrian Jorisz Tienpont, }

William Van Hulst, Vice-Director, ...   1623—   1624

Peter Minuit, Director-General, .   1624—   1632

Giles Osset, Commissary, (killed by the Indians,) . . . .   1630—   1632

Wouter Van Twiller, Director-General, ... April —, 1633—Mar. 28, 1638

Arent Corssen, Vice-Director, .   1633—   1635

Jan Jansen Van Ilpendam, Commissary, ...   1635—   1638

Sir William Keift, Director-General, Mar. 28, 1638—May 27, 1647

Jan Jansen Van Ilpendam, Vice-Director, ... 1638—Oct. 12, 1645

Andreas Hudde, Vice-Director, Oct. 12, 1645—Aug. 15, 1648

Alexander Beyer, acting Commissary, ... Aug. 15, 1648—   1649

Peter Stuyvesant, Director-General, May 17, 1647—May 31, 1654

Gerrit Bricker, Commissary, . .   1649—   1654

[Captured by the Swedes, May 31, 1654.]

GOVERNORS OF NEW SWEDEN, AND OF THE SWEDES ON THE DELAWARE.

Peter Minuit, Governor, ... April 28, 1638—Jan. 30, 1640

Jost de Bogardt, acting Governor, . Jan. 30, 1640—Oct. 15, 1640

Peter Hollandare, Governor, . . . Oct. 15, 1640—Feb. 15, 1643

John Printz, Governor . . . . . . Feb. 15, 1643—Nov. 1, 1653

Hendrick Huygen, Commissary,   1646—

John Pappegoya, acting Governor, . Nov. —, 1653—May 27, 1654

John Claudius Rysingh, Governor, . May 27, 1654—May 31, 1654

9

OFFICERS OF THE

DIRECTORS OF THE ENGLISH OR NEW HAVEN COL-
ONY ON SOUTH RIVER.

Thomas Lamberton, ...   1641—   1653
[Colony expelled by the Dutch and Swedes, 1653.]

DOMINION OF THE SWEDES.

John Claudius Rysingh, Governor, . May 31, 1654—Sept. 25, 1655
Hendrick Van Elswyck, Factor
and Secretary, ... May 31, 1654—Sept. 25, 1655
[Captured by the Dutch, September 25, 1655.]

DOMINION OF THE DUTCH.

Peter Stuyvesant, Director-General, Sept. 25, 1655—Oct.   1, 1664
John Paul Jacquet, Vice-Direc-
tor, ... Nov. 29, 1655—Dec. 19, 1656
Capt. Deryck Smidt, Commissary Oct. —, 1655—Nov. 29, 1655
Andreas Hudde, Commissary, . Dec.   3, 1655—Sept. 23, 1659
Cornelis Van Ruyven, Commis-
sary, ... Sept. 23, 1659—
[The Colony divided into that of the City and Company, 1656.]
COLONY OF THE CITY :
Jacob Alricks, [died Dec. 30,
1659,] . . . . Dec. 19, 1656—Dec. 30, 1659
Alexander D'Hinayossa, ... Dec. 30, 1659—Dec. 22, 1663
COLONY OF THE COMPANY :
Gerrit [Goeran] Van Dyck,
schout-fiscal, ... Jan. —, 1657—Oct. 28, 1658
William Beekman, Vice-Govern-
or, ... Oct. 28, 1658—Dec. 22, 1663
[Colonies of the City and Company united, Dec. 22, 1663.]
Alexander D'Hinayossa, Vice-
Director, ... Dec. 22, 1663—Oct.   1, 1664
[Captured by the English, 1664.]

10

COLONIES ON THE DELAWARE.

DOMINION OF THE DUKE OF YORK.

Col. Richard Nicolls, Governor, . . Sept. 3, 1664—May —, 1667
  Sir Robert Carr, Deputy Govern-
    or, ... Oct. 1, 1664—Nov. 3, 1667
Col. Francis Lovelace, Governor, . May —, 1667—July 30, 1673
  Capt. John Carr, Deputy Gov-
    ernor, ... 1668—July 30, 1673
      [Re-captured by the Dutch, July 30, 1673.]

DOMINION OF THE DUTCH.

Anthony Colve, Governor General, Aug. 12, 1673—Nov. 10, 1674
Peter Alricks, Deputy Governor, Sept. 19, 1673—Nov. 10, 1674
      [Re-taken by the English, Nov. 10, 1674.]

DOMINION OF THE ENGLISH.

Sir Edmund Andros, Governor, . . Nov. 10, 1674—Jan. 16, 1681
  Capt. Matthias Nicolls, Deputy
    Governor, ... Nov. 10, 1674—   1675
  Capt. Edmund Cantwell, Deputy
    Governor, ...   1675—   1676
  Capt. John Collier, Deputy Gov-
    ernor, ...   1676—   1677
  Capt. Christopher Billop, Depu-
    ty Governor, ...   1677—   1680
Capt. Anthony Brockholls, Governor, Jan. 16, 1681—June 21, 1681
[Colonial Government ceases by virtue of Provincial Charter of
March 14, 1681.]

OFFICERS OF THE DUTCH ON THE DELAWARE.

Council:
  Alexander D'Hinayossa, ... 1658
  Abraham Rynvelt, (died Oct. 28, 1658,) 1658
  Gerrit Van Sweringen, ... Oct. 28, 1858
  Cornelis Van Gezel, (removed,) 1660
  John Prato, ... Jan. 25, 1660

11

Commander on the Whorekill:
Peter Alricks, ... Jan.   —, 1660

Schepens:
John Williamson, ... 1659
John Prato, ... 1659
Hendrick Kipp, ... 1659
Jacobus Backer, ... Mar.   —, 1660

Sheriffs or Schouts:
Gregorius Van Dyck, ... May   20, 1657
Gerrit Van Sweringen, ... 1660

Overseers of Fences:
Harman Jansen, ... Nov.   4, 1656
John Eckhart, ... Nov.   4, 1656

Inspectors of Tobacco:
Meenes Andriessen, ... Dec.   12, 1656
William Maunts, ... Dec.   12, 1656

Magistrates for the South River:
Oloff Stille, ... 1657
Mathys Hanson, ... 1657
Peter Rambo, ... 1657
Peter Cock, ... 1657

Officers over the Swedes.
Swen Schute, captain, ... 1658
Andries Dalbo, lieutenant, ... 1658
Jacob Swensen, ensign, ... 1659
Martin Krygier, captain, ... Sept.   22, 1659

Commissioners to Maryland:
Augustine Herman, ... Sept.   23, 1659
Resolved Waldron, ... Sept.   23, 1659

OFFICERS OF THE COLONY OF THE CITY.

Assistant Commissaries:
Hendrick Kipp, ... June   26, 1660
Jacob Crabbe, ... June   26, 1660
Jaes Jonsten, ... June   26, 1660

Collector of Tolls:
Peter Cock, ... Sept.   9, 1663

12

COLONIES ON THE DELAWARE.

Surveyor:
  William Rosenbery, ... Feb. 20, 1661
Surgeon:
  —— Williams, ... April —, 1660
Secretaries:
  Gerrit Van Gezel, ... Dec. 30, 1659 to Aug. —, 1660
  John Prato, assistant, ... Aug. —, 1660
  Gerrit Van Sweringen, assistant, ... Aug. —, 1660

OFFICERS OF THE COLONY OF THE COMPANY.

Assistant Commissaries:
  Peter Rambo, (resigned March, 1661.)
Surgeon:
  Peter Tyneman, ... April —, 1660
Sheriff:
  Gerrit Van Dyck, (removed May 1661.)

OFFICERS FOR THE WHOREKILL.

[Town and county of Whorekill changed to Deal, December 25, 16¨0.]

Commissaries:
  Sander Molleston, ... Mar. 10, 1670
  Oelle Wolgart, ... Mar. 10, 1670
  William Claessen, ... Mar. 10, 1670
  Oelle Wolgart, ... July —, 1672
  William Claessen, ... July —, 1672
  Isaac Jarey, ... July —, 1672

Sheriffs:
  Hermanus Frederickson, ... Feb. 28, 1669
  Hermanus Wiltbank, ... Aug. 1, 1672
  John Vines, ... July 12, 1679

Collector of Customs:
  Martin Krygier, ... Mar. 15, 1669

Surveyors :

James Mills, ... Jan.   9, 1670
Cornelius Verhoof, ... July 12, 1679

Clerks of Courts :

Cornelius Verhoof, ... 1680
William Clarke, ... April 9, 1681

Officers of Company of Foot :

John Avery, captain, ... Oct. 26, 1676
John Roach, ensign, ... Oct. 26, 1676

Justices :

Hermanus Wiltbank, ... Nov. 28, 1673
Alexander Molleston, ... Nov. 28, 1673
Dr. John Rhoades, ... Nov. 28, 1673
William Claessen, ... Nov. 28, 1673
Hermanus Wiltbank, ... Oct. 26, 1676
Edward Southern, ... Oct. 26, 1676
Alexander Molleston, ... Oct. 26, 1676
John King, ... Oct. 26, 1676
Paul Mush, ... Oct. 26, 1676
Hermanus Wiltbank, ... Nov. 20, 1676
Henry Smith, ... Nov. 20, 1676
Alexander Molleston, ... Nov. 20, 1676
Edward Southern, ... Nov. 20, 1676
Paul Mush, ... Nov. 20, 1676
John Barkstead, ... Nov. 20, 1676
John Rhoades, ... Nov. 20, 1676
John Avery, ... Oct. 18, 1678
Francis Whitwell, ... Oct. 18, 1678
John Kipsham, ... Oct. 18, 1678
Luke Watson, ... Oct. 18, 1678
John Rhoades, ... Oct. 18, 1678
James Wells, ... Oct. 18, 1678
Luke Watson, ... June 7, 1680
John Rhoades, ... June 7, 1680
John Kipsham, ... June 7, 1680
Otto Wolgart, ... June 7, 1680
William Clarke, ... June 7, 1680

OFFICERS FOR NEW CASTLE ON DELAWARE.

Sheriff:
Edward Cantwell, ... Aug. 12, 1672
Under Sheriffs:
George More, ... 1676
Thomas Molleston, ... 1677
Bailiff:
Peter Alricks, ... Aug. 12, 1672
Clerks of Courts:
William Tom, ... Nov. 14, 1674
Ephraim Herman, ... Oct. 3, 1676
Collectors of Customs:
John DeHaas, ... Nov. 14, 1674
John Collier, ... Sept. 23, 1676
Christopher Billop, ... Aug. 23, 1677
Constables:
Walter Rowles, ... Aug. 24, 1677
Erick Cock, ... Oct. 23, 1680
Surveyor:
Philip Pocock, (died June, 1680,) . . . . Dec. 25, 1678
Ephraim Herman, ... June 22, 1680
Overseers of Highways:
John Cock, ... Oct. 23, 1680
Lasse Dalbo, ... Oct. 23, 1680
Justices:
Hans Block, ... Nov. —, 1674
John Moll, ... Nov. —, 1674
Foppe Oothout, ... Nov. —, 1674
Joseph Chew, ... Nov. —, 1674
Dirck Alberts, ... Nov. —, 1674
John Moll, ... Oct. 3, 1676
Henry Ward, ... Oct. 3, 1676
William Tom, ... Oct. 3, 1676
Foppe Oothout, ... Oct. 3, 1676
John Paul Jacquet, ... Oct. 3, 1676
Garritt Otto, ... Oct. 3, 1676
John Moll, ... Oct. 16, 1677
Peter Alricks, ... Oct. 16, 1677
William Tom, (died 1681,) . . . . Oct. 16, 1677
Foppe Oothout, ... Oct. 16, 1677

15

Walter Wharton, (died Dec. —, 1678,)	Oct.	16, 1677
John Paul Jacquet,	Oct.	16, 1677
John Moll, president,	Nov.	7, 1678
Peter Alricks,	Nov.	7, 1678
Foppe Oothout,	Nov.	7, 1678
Garritt Otto,	Nov.	7, 1678
Johannes De Haas,	Nov.	7, 1678
Abraham Mann,	Nov.	7, 1678
William Semple,	Nov.	7, 1678
John Moll,	June.	7, 1680
Peter Alricks,	June	7, 1680
Garritt Otto,	June	7, 1680
Johannes De Haas,	June	7, 1680
William Semple,	June	7, 1680

OFFICERS FOR UPLAND AND DEPENDENCIES.

Justices:

Peter Cock,	Nov.	—, 1674
Peter Rambo,	Nov.	—, 1674
Israel Helm,	Nov.	—, 1674
Lace Andries,	Nov.	—, 1674
Oelle Swensen,	Nov.	—, 1674
Peter Cock,	Oct.	3, 1676
Peter Rambo,	Oct.	3, 1676
Israel Helm,	Oct.	3, 1676
Lace Andries,	Oct.	3, 1676
Oelle Swensen,	Oct.	3, 1676
Otto Ernest Cock,	Oct.	3, 1676
Otto Ernest Cock,	May	28, 1680
Israel Helm,	May	28, 1680
Lasse Cock,	May	28, 1680
Henry James,	May	28, 1680
George Browne,	May	28, 1680
William Clayton,		1681
William Warner,		1681
Robert Wade,		1681
William Byles,		1681
Robert Lucas,		1681
Thomas Fairman,		1681
James Sandelands,		1681
Swen Swensen,		1681
Andries Bankson,		1681

COLONIES ON THE DELAWARE.

Surveyors:

Walter Wharton,	1676
Richard Noble,	Dec. 15, 1679

Clerks of Upland Court:

William Tom,	1674
Ephraim Herman,	1676

Collector of Quit-Rent:

Ephraim Herman,	Aug. 23, 1677

Sheriff:

Edward Cantwell,	Nov. —, 1676

Under Sheriffs:

Jurien Hartswelder,	Nov. —, 1676
Michael Yzard,	Sept. 11, 1677
William Warner,	1679

Constable:

Albert Hendricks,	1676
William Orian,	Sept. 11, 1677
Andries Homman,	June 18, 1678
William Coyles, "att ye faals,"	1680

OFFICERS FOR ST. JONES AND DEPENDENCIES.

Justices:

Francis Whitwell,	June 7, 1680
John Hilliard,	June 7, 1680
Robert Hart,	June 7, 1680
Edward Pack,	June 7, 1680

OFFICERS UNDER THE DUKE OF YORK.

Commissioners:

Sir Robert Carr, Knt.,	May 5, 1664
George Carteret,	May 5, 1664
Samuel Maverick, Esq.,	May 5, 1664

17

OFFICERS OF THE

Councillors:

John Carr,	May	—, 1667
Hans Block,	May	—, 1667
Israel Helm,	May	—, 1667
Peter Rambo,	May	—, 1667
Peter Cock,	May	—, 1667
Peter Alricks,	May	—, 1667

Indian Trader:

Peter Gronendyke, (at the Whorekill,)	Nov.	1, 1670

Surveyor General West Side of Delaware:

Walter Wharton,	June	27, 1671

Commander in Delaware Bay and River:

John Collier,	Sept.	23, 1676

Commissioners to Appraise the Island of Tinicum:

Peter Alricks,	Mar.	2, 1673
Edmund Cantwell,	Mar.	2, 1673
William Tom,	Mar.	2, 1673
Walter Wharton,	Mar.	2, 1673

OFFICERS OF THE PRO-PROVINCIAL GOVERNMENT.

[Nov. 25, 1682, The Province divided into three counties, and Territories into three. Dec. 25, 1682, Deal changed to Sussex, Jones to Kent.]

William Penn, Proprietary and Governor,	Mar.	14, 1681
William Markham, Deputy Governor,	April	20, 1681

Overseers of Highways:

Wooley Rawson, from Marcus creek to Naaman's creek.
William Oxley, from Upland creek to Ammersland's creek.
Mins Staukett, from Ammersland's creek to Karkus mill.
Peter Yokeham, from Karkus mill to Schorekill Falls.
Andreas Rambo, from Schorekill Falls to Tawcony creek.
Erick Mullikey, from Tawcony creek to Poquessink creek.
Claus Johnson, from Poquessink creek to Samuel Cliff's.
John Akraman, from Samuel Cliff's to Gilbert Wheeler's.
William Biles, ... June 14, 1681
Richard Noble, Surveyor for Upland.

Commissioners appointed by Penn for the Colony.

William Crispin,	Oct.	10, 1681
John Bezar,	Oct.	10, 1681
Nathaniel Allen,	Oct.	10, 1681

18

COLONIES ON THE DELAWARE.

Surveyor General:
    Capt. Thomas Holmes, ... April 18, 1682

Assistant Surveyor General:
    John Claypoole.

Justices for Newcastle:
    John Moll, ... ⎫
    Peter Alricks, ... ⎪
    Johannes De Haas, ... ⎪
    William Semple, ... ⎬ Oct. 28, 1682
    Arnoldus de la Grange, ... ⎪
    John Cann, ... ⎭

Peter Bancomb, Sheriff St. Jones county, ... 1682
John Vines, Sheriff Whorekill or Deal, ... Nov. 18, 1682

PROVINCIAL COUNCILLORS OF CHESTER COUNTY.

John Simcock, three years, ... Nov. —, 1682
Ralph Withers, two years, ... Nov. —, 1682
William Clayton, one year, ... Nov. —, 1682

OFFICERS OF UPLAND COURT.

Justices:
    William Clayton, ... Sept. 13, 1681
    William Warner, ... Sept. 13, 1681
    Robert Wade, ... Sept. 13, 1681
    Otto Ernest Cock, ... Sept. 13, 1681
    William Biles, ... Sept. 13, 1681
    Robert Lucas, ... Sept. 13, 1681
    Lasse Cock, ... Sept. 13, 1681
    Swen Swenson, ... Sept. 13, 1681
    Andrew Bankson, ... Sept. 13, 1681
    James Sandelands, ... Nov. 30, 1681
    Thomas Fairman, ... Nov. 30, 1681
    Hendricks Bankson, ... Nov. 30, 1681

Sheriff:
    John Test, ... Sept. 13, 1681

Clerk:
    Thomas Revell, ... Sept. 13, 1681

OFFICERS

OF THE

PROVINCE OF PENNSYLVANIA.

1681—1776.

OFFICERS OF THE PROVINCE.

GOVERNORS OF THE PROVINCE.

WILLIAM PENN, PROPRIETARY, . 1681—   1693
William Markham, Deputy Gov-
 ernor, ... April 20, 1681—Oct. —, 1682
William Penn, Proprietary and
 Governor, ... Oct. 27, 1682—Sept. 18, 1684
The Council, (Thomas Lloyd,
 President, ... Sept. 18, 1684—Feb. 9, 1688
1. Thomas Lloyd,
2. Robert Turner, Five Commis-
3. Arthur Cook, sioners ap- Feb. 9, 1688—Dec. 18, 1688
4. John Simcock, pointed by
      Wm. Penn.
5. John Eckley,
Capt. John Blackwell, Deputy
 Governor, ... Dec. 18, 1688—Jan. 2, 1690
The Council, (Thomas Lloyd,
 President,) . . . . Jan. 2, 1690—Mar. —, 1691
Thomas Lloyd, Deputy Gov-
 ernor of Province, ...
William Markham, Deputy Mar. —, 1691—April 26, 1693
 Governor of Lower Counties,

CROWN OF ENGLAND, ... 1693—Nov. 24, 1694
Benjamin Fletcher, Governor of
 New York, Governor, ... April 26, 1693—Mar. 26, 1695
William Markham, Lieutenant
 Governor, ... April 26, 1693—Mar. 26, 1695

WILLIAM PENN, PROPRIETARY, . Nov. 24, 1694—July 30, 1718
William Markham, Governor, . Mar. 26, 1695 - Sept. 3, 1698
Samuel Carpenter, Deputies, Nov. 24, 1694—Sept. 3, 1698
John Goodson,
William Markham, Lieutenant
 Governor, ... Sept. 3, 1698—Dec. 21, 1699

23

OFFICERS OF THE

William Penn, Proprietary and
  Governor, ... Dec. 21, 1699—Oct. 27, 1701
Andrew Hamilton, Deputy Gov-
  ernor, ... Oct. 27, 1701—April 20, 1703
The Council, (Edward Shippen,
  President,) . . . . April 20, 1703—Feb.   3, 1704
John Evans, Deputy Governor, . Feb. 3, 1704—Feb.   1, 1709
Charles Gookin, Deputy Govern-
  or, ... Feb. 1, 1709—May 31, 1717
Sir William Keith, Deputy Gov-
  ernor, ... May 31, 1717—July 30, 1718

JOHN PENN, RICHARD PENN, and
  THOMAS PENN, Proprietaries, . .   1718—   1746
Sir William Keith, Deputy Gov-
  ernor, ... July 30, 1718—June 22, 1726
Patrick Gordon, Deputy Govern-
  or, ... June 22, 1726—Aug.   4, 1736
The Council, (James Logan, Pres-
  ident,) . . . . Aug. 4, 1736—June   1, 1738
George Thomas, Deputy Govern-
  or, ... June 1, 1738—May   —, 1746

RICHARD PENN and THOMAS PENN,
  Proprietaries, ...   1746—   1771
George Thomas, Deputy Govern-
  or, ... May —, 1746—May 29, 1747
The Council, (Anthony Palmer,
  President,) . . . . May 29, 1747—Nov. 23, 1748
James Hamilton, Deputy Gov-
  ernor, ... Nov. 23, 1748—Oct.   3, 1754
Robert Hunter Morris, Deputy
  Governor, ... Oct.   3, 1754—Aug. 25, 1756
William Denny, Deputy Gov-
  ernor, ... Aug. 25, 1756—Nov. 17, 1759
James Hamilton, Deputy Gov-
  ernor, ... Nov. 17, 1759—Oct. 31, 1763
John Penn, (son of Richard
  Penn,) Deputy Governor, . . Oct. 31, 1763—May   4, 1771

THOMAS PENN and JOHN PENN,
  (son of Richard,) Proprietaries, .   1771—   1776
The Council, (James Hamilton,
  President,) . . . . May   4, 1771—Oct. 16, 1771

24

PROVINCE OF PENNSYLVANIA.

Richard Penn, (son of Richard
  Penn,) Lieutenant Governor, Oct. 16, 1771—July 19, 1773
The Council, (James Hamilton,
  President,) . . . . July 19, 1773—Aug. 30, 1773
John Penn, Governor, ... Aug. 30, 1773—Sept. 28, 1776
[August 30, 1773, John Penn, who was confirmed Lieutenant Governor by the King, June 30, was awarded the title of Governor by the Provincial Council.]

=========

MEMBERS OF THE GOVERNOR'S COUNCIL, 1683—1776.

Allen, Andrew, (died 1825,) 1770–76
Alricks, Peter, Newcastle, ... 1685–89
Assheton, Ralph, (died 1745,) 1728–45
Assheton, Robert, (died 1727,) 1711–27
Assheton, William, ... 1722–23
Barnes, John, Bucks, ... 1685–87
Bedwell, Thomas, ... 1700
Biles, William, Bucks, ... 1683, 1695, 1698–1700
Blunston, John, Chester, resigned, (died
  1723,) 1690
Brinkloe, John, Kent, ... 1690, 1695–6
Bristow, John, Chester, (died 1694,) . . 1687–92
Cadwalader, Thomas, (died 1779,) . . . 1755–76
Cann, John, Newcastle, ... 1684–93
Cantwell, Edmund, Newcastle, ... 1683–84
Carpenter, Samuel, Philadelphia, . . . 1687–89, 1695, 1697–1713
Chew, Benjamin, ... 1755–76
Clarke, William, Sussex, ... 1683–1705
Claypoole, James, Philadelphia, (died
  1687,) 1687
Clayton, William, Chester, ... 1683–84
Clifton, Robert, Sussex, ... 1695
Clifton, Thomas, Sussex, ... 1690
Cock, Lasse, ... 1683
Cock, Lawrence, Philadelphia, ... 1693
Cook, Arthur, Bucks, ... 1686–88, 1690
Coppock, Bartholomew, Chester, (died
  1720,) 1688–90
Curtis, John, Kent, ... { 1687 (not then admitted) 1689–90, 1697–98
Darnall, William, Kent, ... 1684–88
Delarall, John, ... 1692
De Haas, John, Newcastle, ... 1688–90

25

Dickinson, Jonathan, (died 1722,) . . . 1711, 1722
Donaldson, John, Newcastle, ... 1695-96, 1698-1700
Duckett, Thomas, Philadelphia, ... 1690
Dyer, William, Sussex, ... 1687 (not admitted)
Eckley, John, Philadelphia, (died 1689,) 1688-89
Fenwick, Thomas, Sussex, ... 1700
Finney, John, ... 1702
Finney, Samuel, ... 1701
Fishbourne, William, (dismissed,) . . . 1723-31
Foreman, George, ... 1693-94
Frampton, William, Kent, (died 1686,) . 1685-86
French, John, (died 1728,) 1717-28
French, Robert, ... 1700
Graeme, Thomas, (dropped,) (died 1772,) 1726-38
Green, Edward, Newcastle, ... 1685-86
Griflitts, Thomas, ... 1733-42
Growden, Joseph, Bucks, ... 1687-89, 1692, 1695, 1697-98
Growden, Lawrence, (died 1770,) . . . 1747-1770
Guest, John, ... 1701-7
Haige, William, ... 1683
Hallowell, Richard, Newcastle, . . . 1695-1700
Hamilton, Andrew, (died 1741,) 1720-41
Hamilton, James, (died 1783,) 1745-76
Harrison, Francis, Chester, ... 1686
Harrison, James, Bucks, ... 1683
Hassell, Samuel, (died 1751,) 1728-51
Hicks, William, (died 1776,) 1771-76
Hill, John, Sussex, ... 1689, 1696-1700
Hill, Richard, ... 1704-28
Hilliard, John, ... 1683
Holmes, Thomas, ... 1683
Hough, Richard, Bucks, ... 1692, 1700
Howell, William, (did not serve,) . . . 1690
Janney, Thomas, ... 1683-86
Jones, Griffith, Kent, ... 1687-90, 1695-97
Lardner, Lynford, (died 1773,) 1755-73
Lawrence, Thomas, (died 1753,) . . . 1727-53
Levis, Samuel, (died 1728,) 1692
Lloyd, David, Chester, (died 1731,) . . . 1695-1700
Lloyd, Thomas, ... 1684-8
Logan, James, ... 1704-47
Logan, William, (died 1776,) 1747-76
Maris, George, Chester, (died 1703,) . 1695
Markham, William, ... 1683, 1685-89
Masters, Thomas, (died 1726,) 1720-26
Mifflin, John, (died 1759,) 1755-59

26

Moll, John, (died 1701,) 1683, 1700
Molleston, Henry, Kent, ... 1700–1
Mompesson, Roger, ... 1704
Morris, Anthony, (died 1621,) 1695–96
Murray, Humphrey, (died 1716,) 1700–1
Newlin, Nicholas, Chester, (died 1699,) . 1685–87
Norris, Isaac, ... 1709–34
Owen, Evan, ... 1726
Owen, Griffith, Philadelphia, ... 1690–1700
Palmer, Anthony, (died 1748,) 1709–48
Pemberton, Phineas, Philadelphia and
  Bucks, (died 1702,) 1685–87, 1695, 1697–99, 1701
Pemberton, Thomas, Sussex, ... 1695
Penn, William, Jr., ... 1704
Peters, Rev. Richard, (died 1776,) . . . 1749–76
Pidgeon, Joseph, (died 1713,) 1704–8
Plumstead, Clement, ... 1727
Preston, Samuel, ... 1700, 1709–35
Pussey, Caleb, ... 1695, 1697, 1697–1715
Rawle, Francis, (did not serve,)
Read, Charles, (died 1737,) 1733–37
Richardson, John, ... 1883
Richardson, Samuel, Philadelphia, (died
  1719,) 1688, 1695
Rhoades, John, Kent, ... 1683
Roberts, Hugh, ... 1692
Robeson, Andrew, (died 1694,) 1605
Robinson, Patrick, ... 1662–93
Roach, George, ... 1704
Rodney, William, Kent, ... 1688–89
Rolfe, Josiah, ... 1723
Salway, William, (died 1695,) 1693
Sanders, Charles, Philadelphia (died
  1699,) 1694
Shippen, Edward, (died 1712,) 1695–1712
Shippen, Edward, Jr., (died 1806,) . . . 1770–76
Shoemaker, Benjamin, (died 1767,) . . 1745–67
Simcock, John, Chester, (died 1703,) . . 1683–90, 1692, 1697–98, 1700
Southern, Edward, Sussex, ... 1683
Southersby, William, Philadelphia, . . 1684
Stockdale, William, Newcastle, . . . 1689
Story, Thomas, (died 1742,) 1700–6
Strettell, Robert, (died 1761,) 1741–61
Taylor, Abram, (dismissed,) (died 1771,) 1741–51
Taylor, Christopher, ... 1683
Tilghman, James, ... 1767–76

Till, William, (died 1766,) 1741–66
Trent, William, ... 1704
Turner, Joseph, (died 1783,) 1747–76
Turner, Robert, Philadelphia, ... 1686, 1693, 1700
Walker, John, Kent, (did not serve,) . . 1700
Watson, Luke, Newcastle, ... 1683, 1688
Welch, William, (died 1684,) 1683
Whitwell, Francis, (died 1684,) 1683–4
Williams, John, Newcastle, ... 1695
Wilson, Richard, Kent, ... 1695
Withers, Ralph, ... 1683
Wood, William, Chester, (died 1685,) . . 1684–5
Yeates, Jasper, Newcastle, (died 1720,) . 1696–1720
Yardley, William, Bucks, ... 1688

PROPRIETARY SECRETARIES.

Philip T. Lehnman, ... 1683
William Markham, ... May 28, 1685
James Logan, (vice Robinson,) . . . . Oct. 27, 1701
Richard Peters, (vice Logan, deceased,) . . . . . June 6, 1747
Joseph Shippen, Jr., (vice Peters, resigned,) . . . . Jan. 2, 1762

CLERKS OF THE COUNCIL.

Patrick Baird, ... May 20, 1723
Robert Charles, ... Sept. 15, 1726
Thomas Lawrie, ... Aug. 1, 1738
Patrick Baird, (vice Lawrie, resigned,) . . . . . . July 21, 1740
Richard Peters, (vice Baird, resigned,) . . . . . . Feb. 14, 1742–3
Joseph Shippen, Jr., (vice Peters, resigned,) . . . . Jan. 2, 1762

RECEIVERS GENERAL FOR PROPRIETARIES.

John Blackwell, ... Sept. 25, 1689
Samuel Jennings, ... July 15, 1690
Benjamin Chambers, Deputy, ... Nov. 1, 1690
Robert Turner, ... June 1, 1693
James Logan, ... Oct. 29, 1701
Francis Steele, ... Jan. 30, 1714
James Steel, Deputy, ... Mar. 30, 1718

PROVINCE OF PENNSYLVANIA.

James Steel, ... Dec. 16, 1732
Lyndford Lardner, ... Aug. 8, 1741
Richard Hockley, ... Mar. 28, 1753
Edmund Physick, ... Jan. 1, 1769

DEPUTY SURVEYOR OF CHESTER AND LANCASTER.

John Taylor, ... Feb. 1, 173¾

DEPUTY SURVEYOR OF PHILADELPHIA AND BUCKS.

Nicholas Scull, ... Feb. 11, 173¾

REGISTERS GENERAL.

Christopher Taylor, (deceased April, 1686.)
Robert Turner, ⎫
William Frampton, ⎬ acting, ... May 5, 1686
William Southerby, ⎭
James Claypoole, Sr., (deceased June, 1687,) . . . . Sept. 18, 1686
John Eckley, (declined,) . . . . June 18, 1687
Thomas Ellis, ... July 28, 1687
John Blackwell, ... July 25, 1689
Robert Turner, ... Mar. 4, 1690
John Moore, ... Jan. 1, 1693
William Markham, ... March 29, 1703
Benjamin Hayne, William Watson, and Thos. Hay-
          ward lately executed the office, ... 1713
Benjamin Hayne, ... 1712
Peter Evans, ... 1713-15
Thomas Graeme, ... May 14, 1724
Peter Evans, ... Feb. 19, 173½
William Plumsted, ... June 19, 1745
Benjamin Chew, ... Aug. 15, 1765

OFFICERS OF THE

MASTERS OF ROLLS.

Thomas Lloyd, ... Oct.   27, 1683
Patrick Robinson, Deputy, ... •. 1685
William Markham, ... 1690
Thomas Story, ... Feb.   6, 1700
Griffith Owen, Deputy, ... July   11, 1702
Morris Lisle, Deputy, ... April   3, 1705
Charles Brockden, Deputy, ... 1712
Charles Brockden, ... 1722
Andrew Hamilton, ... June   12, 1727
Thomas Hopkinson, ... June   20, 1736
William Allen, ... Aug.   7, 1741
Tench Francis, ... Oct.   2, 1750
Benjamin Chew, ... Aug.   29, 1755
William Parr, ... Sept.   28, 1767
Andrew Allen, ... June   25, 1774

SURVEYORS GENERAL OF THE PROVINCE.

Thomas Holmes, ... April   18, 1682
Thomas Pearson, Deputy, ... July   10, 1684
Thomas Fairman, Deputy, ... 1689
Thomas Holmes, ... 1694
Edward Penington, ... April 26, 1698—1706-7
Jacob Taylor, ... Nov.   20, 1706
Benjamin Eastburn, ... Oct.   29, 1733
William Parsons, of Philadelphia, ... Aug.   22, 1741
Nicholas Scull, ... June   14, 1748
John Lukens, ... Dec.   8, 1761-1776

SECRETARIES OF THE LAND OFFICE.

James Steel.
John Georges, ... April   2, 1733
Richard Peters, ... Nov.   24, 1748
William Peters, ... Nov.   1, 1760
James Tilghman, ... Jan.   1, 1769

30

PROVINCE OF PENNSYLVANIA.

PROVINCIAL TREASURERS.

Samuel Carpenter, deceased, ... June 4, 1704, 1710–11–13
Samuel Preston, deceased, ... 1714–43
Michael Lightfoot, ... 1743–54
Samuel Preston Moore, ... 1755–68
Owen Jones, resigned, ... 1769–76

TRUSTEES OF LOAN OFFICE.

John Wright, ... 1731–2
John Kinsey, ... 173 -43
Jonathan Robeson, ... 173 -43
Joseph Kirkbride, ... 173 -43
Caleb Cowpland, ... 173 -43
Thomas Leech, ... 1743
Benjamin Field, ... 1743
John Owen, ... 1743
Thomas Linley, ... 1743
John Watson, ... 1743
Thomas Chandler, ... 1743
John Wright, ... 1743

PROVINCIAL JUDGES.

Chief Justices.

Arthur Cook, ...	1680—	1684
Nicholas Moore, ...	1684—	1685
James Harrison, (declined,)	1685—	
Arthur Cook, ...	1686—	1690
John Simcock, ...	1690—	1693
Andrew Robson, ...	1693—	1699
Edward Shippen, ...	1699—	1701
John Guest, ... Aug. 20, 1701—April 10, 1703		
William Clark, ... April 10, 1703—		1705
John Guest, ...	1705—	1706
Roger Mompesson, ... April 17, 1706—		1715
Joseph Growden, Jr., ...	1715—	1718
David Lloyd, ...	1718—	1731
Isaac Norris, (declined,) . . . . . April 9, 1731—		
James Logan, ... Aug. 20, 1731—		1739

31

Jeremiah Langhorne, ... Aug. 13, 1739—		1743
John Kinsey, ... April 5, 1743—		1750
William Allen, (vice Kinsey, dec'd,) Sept. 20, 1750—		
Benjamin Chew, ... April 29, 1774—		1776

Puisne Judges.

William Welch, (died July, 1684,) . May 29, 1684—July		—,	1684
William Wood, ... May 29, 1684—July		14,	1685
Robert Turner, ... May 29, 1684—			1685
John Eckley, ... May 29, 1684—			1686
William Clark, (vice Welch,) . . .	1684—		1693
John Claypoole, ...	1685—		1686
Arthur Cook, ...	1685—		1686
John Simcock, ...	1686—		1690
John Cann, ...	1686—		1690
James Harrison, ...	1686—		1690
Joseph Growden, ...	1690—		1693
Peter Alricks, ... Sept 5, 1690—			1693
Thomas Wynn, ... Sept. 5, 1690—			1693
Griffith Jones, ...	1690—		1693
Edward Blake, ...	1690—		1698
William Salway, ...	1693—		1698
John Cann, ...	1693—Aug.	10,	1694
Edward Blake, ...	1693—		1698
Anthony Morris, (vice Cann,) . . . Aug. 10, 1694—			1698
Joseph Growden, ...	1698—		1699
Cornelius Empson, ...	1698—		1701
William Biles, ...	1699—		1701
John Guest, ...	1699—		1701
Joseph Growden, (declined,)	1701—		
Caleb Pusey, (declined,)	1701—		
Thomas Masters, ...	1701—		1705
William Clark, ...	1702—		1703
Capt. Samuel Tinney, ...	1702—		1711
John Guest, ...	1703—		1705
Edward Shippen, ...	1703—		1705
Jasper Yeates, ...	1705—		1711
William Trent, ...	1705—		1711
Joseph Growden, Jr., ...	1705—		1715
George Roche, (resigned,)	1711—		1715
Anthony Palmer, ...	1711—		1715
William Trent, ...	1715—		1722
Jonathan Dickinson, ...	1715—		1718
Robert Asheton, ...	1715—		1718
Richard Hill, ...	1718—		1731
Robert Asheton, ...	1722—		1726

PROVINCE OF PENNSYLVANIA.

William Trent,	1724—(?)	
Jeremiah Langhorne,	1726—	1739
John French, ... July	25, 1726—	
Dr. Thomas Graeme,	1731—	1750
Thomas Griffitts,	1739—	1743
William Till,	1743—	1750
Lawrence Growden,	1750—	1764
Caleb Cowpland, (died 1758,)	1750—	1758
William Coleman, (vice Cowpland,)	1758—	1764
Alexander Stedman,	1764—	1767
John Lawrence,	1767—	1776
Thomas Willing,	1767—	1776
John Morton,	1774—	1776

ATTORNEYS GENERAL FOR THE PROVINCE AND TERRITORIES.

John White,	Oct.	25, 1683
Samuel Hersent, (commission revoked,)	Jan.	16, 1685
John White, (special,)	Nov.	17, 1685
David Lloyd,	April	24, 1686
John Moore,	May	19, 1698
William Assheton,		1700
Par. Parmyter,		1701
George Lowther,	April	5, 1705
Thomas Clarke,	June	24, 1708
Henry Wilson,	Mar.	5, 1717
Andrew Hamilton,	Sept.	24, 1717— 1724
Joseph Growden, Jr., (died 1738,)	Sept.	26, 1726— 1738
John Kinsey,		1738— 1741
Tench Francis,		1741— 1754
Benjamin Chew,		1754— 1769
Andrew Allen,		1769—[1776]

COURT OF CHANCERY.

Chancellors:

    Sir William Keith.
    Patrick Gordon.
    George Thomas.

Masters:

    James Logan, ... Aug. 25, 1720

Jonathan Dickinson, ... Aug. 25, 1720
Samuel Preston, ... Aug. 25, 1720
Richard Hill, ... Aug. 25, 1720
Anthony Palmer, ... Aug. 25, 1720
William Trent, ... Aug. 25, 1720
Thomas Masters, ... Aug. 19, 1721
Robert Assheton, ... Aug. 19, 1721
William Assheton, ... Aug. 19, 1721
John French, ... Aug. 19, 1721
Andrew Hamilton, ... July 30, 1723
Henry Brooke, ... July 30, 1723
William Fishourne, ... June 17, 1725
Thomas Graeme, ... Aug. 4, 1726
Evan Owen, ... Aug. 4, 1726
Thomas Lawrence, ... July 23, 1730
Ralph Assheton, ... July 23, 1730
Samuel Hasel, ... April 8, 1731
Clement Plumstead, ... July 23, 1730

Registers:

Charles Brockden, ... Aug. 25, 1720
Robert Charles, (vice Brockden resigned,) . . . Sept. 1, 1739

Examiners:

Charles Osborne, ... Jan. 22, 172⅔
Patrick Bard, ... Mar. 15, 172⅔

COURT OF VICE ADMIRALTY.

Judges.

William Markham, ... 1693
Robert Quarry, ... 1695
Roger Mompesson, ... 1703
William Assheton, ... 1718
Josiah Rolfe, (sole Judge Vice Admiralty,) . . . June 25, 1724
Joseph Brown, (sole Judge Vice Admiralty,) . . . Mar. 18, 172½
Charles Read, ... April 21, 1735
Andrew Hamilton, ... Sept. 11, 1737
Thomas Hopkinson, ... Jan. 17, 174⅔
Patrick Baird, ... Dec. 12, 1749
Edward Shippen, Jr., ... Nov. 22, 1752–61
George Ross, ... 1776

Deputy Judge.

Isaac Miranda, ... July 19, 1727

PROVINCE OF PENNSYLVANIA.

Clerk of Court.

Patrick Baird, ... June 25, 1724

Advocates.

Joseph Growden, ... April 21, 1735
John Moor, (Deputy Advocate,) 169–

Registers.

Patrick Baird, ... April 21, 1735
William Peters, ... May 2, 1745
William Peters, (Deputy Register,) . . . . June 1, 1743

Commissary.

Robert Jenney, ... May 10, 1743

Judge Commissary and Surrogate.

Jared Ingersoll, ... May 2, 1769

Marshals.

Robert Webb, ... 1693
Richard Brockden, ... April 21, 1735

SURVEYOR OF CUSTOMS.

Patrick Baird, ... 1730

DEPUTY SURVEYOR OF DUTIES AT DELAWARE BAY.

Joseph Shippen, ... Sept. 17, 1760

COLLECTORS OF TONNAGE.

Enoch Story, ... 1762
Richard Pearne, (late Collector,) 1766
Thomas Coombe, ... 1767

PROVINCIAL SECRETARIES.

Richard Ingels, ... 1683
William Markham, ... 1685
David Jamison, ... 1693
Patrick Robinson, ... 1700
James Logan, ... 1703
Robert Assheton, Deputy, ... 1707
Patrick Baird, ... 1723
Robert Charles, ... 1726
John Georges, ... 1733
Robert Charles, ... 1735
Joseph Growden, ... 1736
Thomas Lawrie, ... 1738
Patrick Baird, ... 1740
Richard Peters, ... 1743
Joseph Shippen, ... 1776

KEEPERS OF THE SEAL.

Thomas Lloyd, ... Oct. 20, 1683
Thomas Story, ... June 25, 1700
Edward Shippen, Deputy, ... July 11, 1702
Griffith Owen, Deputy, ... July 11, 1702
James Logan, Deputy, ... July 11, 1702
Thomas Griffitts, ... 1735
Lynford Lardner, ... Dec. 12, 1746
Richard Hockley, ... Mar. 28, 1753
Edmund Physick, ... Jan. 1, 1769

POST-MASTERS GENERAL.

Andrew Hamilton, ... June 4, 1704
John Hamilton, ...
Benjamin Franklin, ... June 1, 1754

PROVINCE OF PENNSYLVANIA.

AGENTS OF PROVINCE TO GREAT BRITAIN.

Ferdinando John Paris, ... 1730–40
Richard Partridge, ... 1740–58
Robert Charles, ... 1756–61
Benjamin Franklin, ... 1757–62
Richard Jackson, ... 1763–65
Benjamin Franklin, ... 1765–75

COMMISSIONERS TO SETTLE DISPUTES WITH CONNECTICUT SETTLERS.

James Burd, (by special commission,) . . . . . June   2, 1763
Thomas McKee, ... June   2, 1763

JUSTICES OF OYER AND TERMINER AND GAOL DELIVERY FOR PHILADELPHIA, BUCKS, AND CHESTER.

Andrew Hamilton, ... Oct. 26, 1730–32
William Allen, ... Oct.   26, 1730
Thomas Graeme, ... April 28, 1732

CLERK OF OYER AND TERMINER AND GAOL DELIVERY.

Joshua Lawrence, ... 1730–1, for divers years past.

NOTARIES AND TABELLIONS PUBLIC AT LARGE.

James Humphreys, ... Jan.   20, 1752
James Humphreys, ... Feb.   22, 1761
Peter Miller, ... Mar.   5, 1765
Paul Fooks, Notary T. P., and Interpreter for Spanish
    and French, ... Sept. 15, 1766
Christian Lehman, ... Dec.   1, 1771

37

James Humphreys,	April 27, 1772
Matthew Clarkson,	April 27, 1772
Peter Miller,	April 27, 1772
John Ord,	April 27, 1772
Paul Fooks, (and sworn Interpreter of French and Spanish,)	Sept. 24, 1776

HEALTH OFFICER.

Spencer Trotter,	1754

INTERPRETER.

Conrad Weiser,	1745

COLLECTOR OF IMPOSTS.

Samuel Holt,	1710–11
Owen Roberts, (on wine,)	1716–23
Charles Read, (collector of excise,)	1724–29

SPEAKERS OF THE ASSEMBLY.

Thomas Wynne,	1682–1683
Nicholas Moore,	1684
John White,	1685–1688
Arthur Cook,	1689
Joseph Growden,	1690–1691
William Clark,	1692
Joseph Growden,	1693
David Lloyd,	1694
Edward Shippen,	1695
John Simcock,	1696
John Blunston,	1697
Phineas Pemberton,	1698
Joseph Blunston,	1699–1700
Joseph Growden,	1701–1703
David Lloyd,	1704–1705

Joseph Growden,	1706
David Lloyd,	1707–1710
Richard Hill,	1711–1712
Isaac Norris,	1713
Joseph Growden,	1714
David Lloyd,	1715
Joseph Growden,	1716
Richard Hill,	1717
William Trent,	1718
John Dickinson,	1719
William Trent,	1720
Isaac Norris,	1721
Jeremiah Langhorne,	1722
Joseph Growden,	1723
David Lloyd,	1724
William Biles,	1725
David Lloyd,	1726–1729
Andrew Hamilton,	1730–1733
Jeremiah Langhorne,	1734
Andrew Hamilton,	1735–1739
John Kinsey,	1740–1745
John Wright,	1746
John Kinsey,	1747
Isaac Norris,	1748–1757
Thomas Leech,	1757
Isaac Norris,	1758–1763
Benjamin Franklin,	1763
Isaac Norris,	1764
Joseph Fox,	1764–1765
Joseph Galloway,	1765–1768
Joseph Fox,	1768
Joseph Galloway,	1769–1774

CLERKS OF ASSEMBLY.

John Claypoole,	1686–88
David Lloyd,	1689–90
William Salway,	1692–94
Francis Cooke,	1695
Stephen Coleman,	1697
Jonathan Dickinson,	1698
Stephen Coleman,	1699
Thomas Makin, (second session,)	1699
Aurelius Hoskins,	1700

Maurice Lisle, ... 1705
William Rakestraw, ... 1706
Thomas Makin, ... 1707
Richard Heath, ... 1710–11
Thomas Wilson, (deceased,) 1711–17
Maurice Lisle, ... 1717–21
Thomas Leech, ... 1723–27
John Roberts, ... 1728–29
Joseph Growden, Jr., ... 1730–36
Benjamin Franklin, ... 1736–50
William Franklin, (resigned,) 1751–57
Thomas Moore, (resigned,) 1757
Charles Moore, ... 1757–76
Abel Evans, Assistant Clerk, ... 1772–76

MESSENGERS OR DOORKEEPERS OF ASSEMBLY.

Richard Reynolds, ... 1686–88
William Ellingworth, ... 1689
George Moore, ... 1690
Charles Ware, ... 1692
Thomas Curtis, ... 1693
Daniel Smith, ... 1697–99
Thomas Woodmanson, (second session,) 1699
William Woodmansey, ... 1700
John Grant, (extra session,) 1700
Nicholas Rosogans, ... 1704–16
Nicholas Rosogans, ... 1717–24
John Campbell, ... 1731–32
John Remington, ... 1732–36
Stephen Fox, ... 1736–37
Stephen Potts, ... 1738–41
Thomas Burden, ... 1742–49
Edward Kelly, ... 1749–55
David Edwards, ... 1755–58
Andrew McNair, ... 1758–76

SERGEANTS-AT-ARMS OF ASSEMBLY.

Peter Worrall, ... 1716–21
John Eyer, ... 1722–28
James Mackey, ... 1728–37
Joseph Prichard, ... 1738–41

PROVINCE OF PENNSYLVANIA.

Samuel Kirk, ... 1741–70
William Sheed, ... 1770–76

KEEPER OF ASSEMBLY LIBRARY.

Charles Norris, . . . - 1754

PROVINCIAL OFFICERS

OF THE

THREE LOWER COUNTIES,

NEW CASTLE, KENT, AND SUSSEX.

NEW CASTLE, KENT, AND SUSSEX.

JUDGES OF SUPREME COURT.

Samuel Lowman, New Castle, ...		1726
Robert Gordon, Kent, ...		1726
Benjamin Shermer, Kent, ...		1726
Henry Brooke, Sussex county, ...		1726
Jonathan Bailey, Sussex, ...		1726

[Also appointed Commissioners of Oyer and Terminer, and General Gaol Delivery in said counties.]

David Evans, ...	April	20, 1727
Richard Grafton, ...	April	20, 1727
Robert Gordon	April	20, 1727
Benjamin Shermer, ...	April	20, 1727
Henry Brooke, ...	April	20, 1727
Jonathan Bailey, ...	April	20, 1727
All Judges now acting re-commissioned, . .	Dec.	1, 1733
John Curtis, ...	April	5, 1743
Thomas Griffits, ...	Aug.	9, 1749
John Vining, (of Kent county,) Chief Justice,	Nov.	2, 1764
Jacob Vanbebber, of New Castle,) 2d Justice,	. Nov.	2, 1764
Richard McWilliams, } 3d Justices, . .	Nov.	2, 1764
John Clowes, (of Sussex,)		
Richard McWilliams, 2d Judge, { Vice Jacob Van-	May	4, 1769
Cæser Rodney, 3d Judge, { bebber and John Clowes, dec'd,	May	4, 1769
Richard McWilliams, Chief Justice, . . .	Oct.	30, 1773
Cæser Rodney, 2d Judge,"	Oct.	30, 1773
Samuel Chew, 3d Judge, ...	Oct.	30, 1773

JUDGES OF OYER AND TERMINER AND GENERAL GAOL DELIVERY.

John Vining, ...	Nov.	27, 1764
Jacob Vanbebber, ...	. Nov.	27, 1764
Richard McWilliams, ...	Nov.	27, 1764
John Vining, ...	. May	4, 1769
Richard McWilliams, ...	May	4, 1769

45

PROVINCIAL OFFICERS OF THE

Cæser Rodney, ... May	4, 1769
Richard McWilliams, ... Nov.	3, 1773
Cæser Rodney, ... Nov.	3, 1773
Samuel Chew, ... Nov.	3, 1773
David Hall, ... Nov.	3, 1773

SPEAKERS OF THE ASSEMBLY OF THE THREE LOWER COUNTIES ON DELAWARE.

Benjamin Chew, ...	1753—1758
Jacob Kollock, ...	1759
John Dickinson, ...	1760
Jacob Kollock, ...	1761—1765
John Vining, ...	1766—1768
Cæser Rodney, ...	1769
John Vining, ...	1770
David Hall, ...	1771
Thomas McKean, ...	1772
Cæser Rodney, ...	1773

TRUSTEES OF THE LOAN OFFICE.

Jacob Kollock, ... May	7, 1759
William Armstrong, ... May	7, 1759
Cæser Rodney, ... May	7, 1759

AGENT OF THE THREE LOWER COUNTIES IN ENGLAND.

David Barclay, Jr., ... April	28, 1760

OFFICERS FOR NEW CASTLE COUNTY.

Sheriff.

Edmund Cantwell, ...	1682
Samuel Laird, ... Feb.	9, 1686
Edward Gibbs, ...	1688
Richard Hallowell, ... Mar.	15, 1690

Edward Lillington,	May 3, 1693
John French,	May 10, 1709
John Gooding,	Oct. 4, 1726–27
William Read,	Oct. 3, 1728–30
John Gooding,	Oct. 4, 1731–32
Henry Newton,	Oct. 4, 1733–34
John Gooding,	Oct. 3, 1735–41
Samuel Bickley,	Oct. 4, 1742–44
Gideon Griffith,	Oct. 5, 1745–46
John Vandyke,	Oct. 8, 1749–50
George Munro,	Oct. 3, 1751–53
William Golden, Sr.,	Oct. 4, 1755
William Golden,	Oct. 5, 1756
John McKinly,	Oct. 4, 1759
Thomas Dunn,	Oct. 3, 1760–62
Thomas Duff,	Oct. 4, 1763–65
John Thompson,	Oct. 4, 1766–68
Thomas Duff,	Oct. 5, 1769–71
John Thompson,	Oct. 5, 1772–74
John Clarke,	Oct. 5, 1775

Coroner.

Robert Robertson,	Feb. 9, 1686
Robert Robinson,	Mar. 15, 1690
Peter Reverdy,	May 3, 1693
Morgan Morgan,	Oct. 4, 1726–29
Abraham Gooding,	Oct. 3, 1730
Robert Robertson,	Oct. 4, 1731
Henry Gum,	Oct. 5, 1732–35
Henry Gum,	Oct. 3, 1741
Benjamin Cook,	Oct. 4, 1742–45
James McMullin,	Oct. 4, 1746
Samuel Silsby,	Oct. 8, 1749–50
John Yeates,	Oct. 3, 1751–52
Robert Morrison,	Oct. 3, 1753–56
William Smith,	Oct. 4, 1759
James Walker,	Oct. 3, 1760–62
William Stewart,	Oct. 4, 1763–64
James Walker,	Oct. 4, 1765–67
William McClay,	Oct. 4, 1768
Henry Vining,	Oct. 5, 1769–71
Joseph Stidham,	Oct. 5, 1772
Robert Bail,	Oct. 4, 1773
Joseph Stidham,	Oct. 5, 1774
Joseph Stidham,	Oct. 5, 1775

Justices for Trial of Negroes.

Evan Rice,	Jan.	25, 1771
David Finney,	Jan.	25, 1771
John Jones,	Dec.	9, 1775
David Finney,	Dec.	9, 1775

Attorneys General at New Castle.

John Ross,	April	26, 1739
George Read, resigned.		
Jacob Moore,	Oct.	20, 1774

Dedimus Potestatem.

Richard McWilliams,	April	10, 1773
George Read,	April	10, 1773
Richard McWilliams,	Oct.	24, 1774
George Read,	Oct.	24, 1774

Clerks.

John White,		1686
John White,		1689
James Claypoole,	May	3, 1693

Clerk of the Peace and Prothonotary.

David French,	Oct.	26, 1728

Clerk of Orphans' Court.

William Read,	Oct.	26, 1728

Register, &c.

John Cann, acting,	Oct.	7, 1685
Robert Gordon,	Oct.	26, 1728

Naval Officer for Port and District of New Castle.

David Finney,	Nov.	4, 1773

Surveyor of Customs from Christiana Creek to Lewistown.

Richard Cantwell,	July	13, 1742

Collectors of Customs at Lewis, now Newcastle.

Samuel Lowman,	Mar. 14, 170$\frac{3}{4}$
Alexander Keith,	Aug. 25, 1729
James Hill,	Mar. 6, 173$\frac{1}{5}$
Henry Brooke, deceased.	
Thomas Forbes, (vice Henry Brooke, deceased,)	April 26, 1738
Rives Holt, (vice Thomas Forbes, deceased,)	Oct. 4, 1738
Richard Metcalfe,	April 28, 1739
Thomas Graeme,	July 6, 1742
John Nelson,	Sept. 26, 1747
William Till, (vice Thomas Graeme, Jr.,)	May 22, 1748

THREE LOWER COUNTIES.

Theodore Maurice, (vice William Till, deceased,) May 27, 1766
James Walker, ... Nov. 13, 1766
Francis Hopkinson, ... May 18, 1772

Deputy Collector of Customs at Newcastle.

Alexander Montgomery, ... Aug. 5, 1772

Comptrollers of Customs at Newcastle.

Christopher Russell, ... Oct. 9, 1764
Theodore Maurice, ... Nov. 2, 1767–70

Ranger.

Peter Alricks, ... , . Feb. 1, 1685

Recorder or Deputy Treasurer.

Samuel Land, ... Feb. 22, 1684

Deputy Surveyors.

John Cann, ... 1684
James Bradshaw, ... July 23, 1685

Trustees of the General Loan Office.

William Patterson, ... May 7, 1759
Richard McWilliams, ... May 7, 1759
Evan Rice, ... , . May 7, 1759
Evan Rice, ... 1764
Richard McWilliams, ... 1764
Thomas McKean, ... : 1764
Evan Rice, ... June 16, 1769
Thomas McKean, ... June 16, 1769
Richard McWilliams, ... June 16, 1769

Signer of Bills of Credit.

William Armstrong, ... May 7, 1759

Chief Burgesses of Wilmington.

William Shipley. . . . . . . Nov. 23, 1739–41
Joseph Way, ... Sept. 11, 1742
William Shipley, ... Sept. 12, 1743
Robert Hannum, . . ' . . Sept. 11, 1744
Joseph Peters, ... Sept. 14, 1745–47
John Stapler, ... Sept. 13, 1748–49
James Few, ... Sept. 12, 1750
Joshua Littler, ... Sept. 10, 1753–54
John Stapler, ... Sept. 14, 1756
John McKinley, ... Sept. 10, 1761
Edward Dawes, ... Sept. 14, 1762–63
John McKinley, ... Sept. 13, 1763
John Lea, ... Sept. 12, 1764

49

Joseph Way, ...	Sept. 12, 1765–66
John McKinley, ...	Sept. 12, 1767–69
Joseph Bennett, ...	Sept. 13, 1770
John McKinley, ...	Sept. 13, 1771–72–73–75

Justices of the Peace.

Peter Alricks, ...	Aug.	22, 1684
Robert Owens, ...	Aug.	22, 1684
Edmund Cantwell, ...	Aug.	22, 1684
Abraham Mann, ...	Aug.	22, 1684
John Cann, ...	Feb.	3, 1685
John De Haas, ...	Feb.	3, 1685
James Williams, ...	Feb.	3, 1685
Hendrick Williams, ...	Feb.	3, 1685
Valentine Hollingsworth, ...	Feb.	3, 1685
Edward Green, ...	Feb.	3, 1685
William Guest, ...	Feb.	3, 1685
Hendrick Lehman, ...	Feb.	3, 1685
Cornelius Empson, ...	July	29, 1685
William Stockdale, ...	July	29, 1685
Edward Blake, ...	July	29, 1685
John Foralt, ...	July	29, 1685
Charles Rumsey, ...	July	29, 1685
Peter Alricks, ...	Jan.	2, 1689
John Cann, ...	Jan.	2, 1689
William Stockdale, ...	Jan.	2, 1689
Edward Blake, ...	Jan.	2, 1689
Cornelius Empson, ...	Jan.	2, 1689
John De Haas, ...	Jan.	2, 1869
Peter Baynton, ...	Jan.	2, 1689
Charles Rumsey, ...	Jan.	2, 1689
Robert Ashton, ...	Jan.	2, 1689
John Hayly, ...	Jan.	2, 1689
Peter Alricks, ...	April	13, 1690
John Cann, ...	April	13, 1690
William Stockdale, ...	April	13, 1690
Edward Blake, ...	April	13, 1690
Cornelius Empson, ...	April	13, 1690
John De Haas, ...	April	13, 1690
Peter Baynton, ...	April	13, 1690
Charles Rumsey, ...	April	13, 1690
Robert Ashton, ...	April	13, 1690
John Hayly, ...	April	13, 1690
Henry Williams, ...	April	13, 1690
Peter Alricks, ...	May	2, 1693

John Donaldson,	May	2, 1693
Richard Hallowell,	May	2, 1693
John Grubb,	May	2, 1693
John Cann,	May	2, 1693
Edward Blake,	May	2, 1693

[Under Governor Fletcher, in 1693, the commissions of all justices of the peace were abrogated, and the members of his council were qualified as justices for the Province and Territories. [*Col. Rec., vol. i, p. 368.*]

John French,	May	14, 1724
John French,	July	25, 1726
Robert Gordon,	July	25, 1726
Joseph England,	July	25, 1726
Charles Springer,	July	25, 1726
John Richardson,	July	25, 1726
James James,	July	25, 1726
William Battell,	July	25, 1726
David Evans,	July	25, 1726
Andrew Peterson,	July	25, 1726
Ebenezer Empson,	July	25, 1726
Hans Hanson,	July	25, 1726
James Dyer,	July	25, 1726
Samuel Kirk,	July	25, 1726
Richard Grafton,	July	25, 1726
Simon Hadley,	July	25, 1726
Robert Gordon,	April	20, 1727
John Richardson,	April	20, 1727
Joseph England,	April	20, 1727
Charles Springer,	April	20, 1727
Andrew Peterson,	April	20, 1727
Hans Hanson,	April	20, 1727
Simon Hadley,	April	20, 1727
William Read,	April	20, 1727
Thomas January,	April	20, 1727
James James, Jr.,	April	20, 1727
Richard Cantwell,	April	20, 1727
Joseph Robinson,	April	20, 1727
James Armitage,	April	20, 1727
All Justices now acting re-commissioned,	Dec.	1, 1733
Members of Pr'y and Governor's Council,	Nov.	1, 1764
Evan Rice,	Nov.	1, 1764
Thomas James,	Nov.	1, 1764
William Patterson,	Nov.	1, 1764
William Armstrong,	Nov.	1, 1764

John Jones,	Nov.	1, 1764
William Williams,	Nov.	1, 1764
Richard McWilliams,	Nov.	1, 1764
John Stapler,	Nov.	1, 1764
David Finney,	Nov.	1, 1764
Thomas Cooch,	Nov.	1, 1764
James Latimer,	Nov.	1, 1764
Thomas McKim,	Nov.	1, 1764
Jacob Peterson,	Nov.	1, 1764
John Evans,	Nov.	1, 1764
Thomas Tobin,	Nov.	1, 1764
Theodore Maurice,	Nov.	1, 1764
The members of Council,	Oct.	28, 1769
Evan Rice,	Oct.	28, 1769
John Stapler,	Oct.	28, 1769
Thomas James,	Oct.	28, 1769
David Finney,	Oct.	28, 1769
William Patterson,	Oct.	28, 1769
Thomas Cooch,	Oct.	28, 1769
William Armstrong,	Oct.	28, 1769
James Latimer,	Oct.	28, 1769
John Jones,	Oct.	28, 1769
Thomas McKim,	Oct.	28, 1769
William Williams,	Oct.	28, 1769
Jacob Peterson,	Oct.	28, 1769
John Evens,	Oct.	28, 1769
Thomas Tobin,	Oct.	28, 1769
Theodore Maurice,	Oct.	28, 1769
Thomas McKean,	Oct.	28, 1769
Benjamin Noxon,	Oct.	28, 1769
John Malcolm,	Oct.	28, 1769
John Jones,	April	10, 1773
Thomas James,	April	10, 1773
William Patterson,	April	10, 1773
William Armstrong,	April	10, 1773
William Williams,	April	10, 1773
John Stapler,	April	10, 1773
David Finney,	April	10, 1773
Thomas Cooch,	April	10, 1773
James Latimer,	April	10, 1773
Thomas McKim,	April	10, 1773
Jacob Peterson,	April	10, 1773
John Evans,	April	10, 1773
Theodore Maurice,	April	10, 1773
Thomas McKean,	April	10, 1773
Benjamin Noxon,	April	10, 1773

John Malcolm,	April	10, 1773
George Craighead,	April	10, 1773
Richard Cantwell,	April	10, 1773
Members of Council,	Oct.	24, 1774
John Jones,	Oct.	24, 1774
Thomas James,	Oct.	24, 1774
William Patterson,	Oct.	24, 1774
John Stapler,	Oct.	24, 1774
David Finney,	Oct.	24, 1774
Thomas Cooch,	Oct.	24, 1774
James Latimer,	Oct.	24, 1774
Thomas McKim,	Oct.	24, 1774
John Evans,	Oct.	24, 1774
Theodore Maurice,	Oct.	24, 1774
Thomas McKean,	Oct.	24, 1774
Benjamin Noxon,	Oct.	24, 1774
John Malcolm,	Oct.	24, 1774
George Craighead,	Oct.	24, 1774
Richard Cantwell,	Oct.	24, 1774
Samuel Patterson,	Oct.	24, 1774
John Thompson,	Oct.	24, 1774
Abraham Robinson,	Oct.	24, 1774

Assembly.

John Cann,	1682–83
John Darby,	1682–83
Valentine Hollingsworth,	1682–83
Gasparus Herman,	1682–83
John De Haas,	1682–83
James Williams,	1682–83
William Guest,	1682–83
Peter Alricks,	1682–83
Hendrick Williams,	1682–83
James Williams,	1684
John Darby,	1684
William Grant,	1684
Gasparus Herman,	1684
Abraham Mann,	1684
John White,	1684
John White, (Speaker,)	1685
Gasparus Herman,	1685
Hendrick Williams,	1685
Abraham Mann,	1685
Edward Owen, Jr.,	1685
John Darby,	1685
John White, (Speaker,)	1686

John Darby, ... 1686
Cornelius Empson, ... 1686
James Williams, ... 1686
Abraham Mann, ... 1686
William Grant, ... 1686
Johannes De Haas, ... 1687
Edward Blake, ... 1687
Valentine Hollingsworth, ... 1687
John White, (Speaker,) 1687
John Darby, ... 1687
Richard Noble, ... 1687
John White, (Speaker,) 1688
Edward Blake, ... 1688
Peter Baynton, ... 1688
Valentine Hollingsworth, ... 1688
John Darby, ... 1688
Joseph Holding, [Holden,] 1688
John Darby, ... 1689
John White, (in prison,) 1689
Valentine Hollingsworth, ... 1689
Edward Blake, ... 1689
Isaac Weldon, [Welden,] 1689
Richard Mankin, ... 1689
Edward Blake, ... 1690
Harry Williams, ... 1690
Richard Hallowell, ... 1690
John Darby, ... 1690
William Grant, ... 1690
John Donaldson, ... 1690
John Darby, ... 1692
John Donaldson, ... 1692
Joseph England, ... 1692
John Grubb, ... 1692
Robert Ashton, ... 1692
Edward Blake, ... 1692
Edward Blake, ... 1693
Cornelius Empson, ... 1693
Henry Williams, ... 1693
Richard Hallowell, ... 1693
John Donaldson, ... 1694
Edward Blake, ... 1694
Richard Hallowell, ... 1694
Henry Williams, ... 1694
Joseph England, ... 1695
Valentine Hollingsworth, ... 1695
George Harland, ... 1695

Edward Gibbs, ... 1695
Henry Hollingsworth, ... 1695
Cornelius Empson, ... 1695
John Hussey, ... 1696
Cornelius Empson, ... 1696
George Hogg, ... 1696
Adam Peterson, ... 1696
Cornelius Empson, ... 1697
Benjamin Grundy, ... 1697
John Richardson, ... 1697
John Buckley, ... 1697
Adam Peterson, ... 1698
Edward Gibbs, ... 1698
John Grubb, ... 1698
Joseph England, ... 1698
None returned, ... 1699
Adam Peterson, (special session, eleventh month,) . 1699
John Healy, ... 1699
William Houston, ... 1699
William Guest, ... 1699
Adam Peterson, ... 1700
Joseph England, ... 1700
Richard Cantwell, ... 1700
William Houston, ... 1700
Robert French, ... 1700
Valentine Hollingsworth, ... 1700
John Healy, (extra session,) 1700
Richard Hallowell, (extra session,) 1700
Robert French, (extra session,) 1700
Jasper Yeates, (extra session,) 1700
Jasper Yeates, ... 1701
John Donaldson, ... 1701
Richard Hallowell, ... 1701
Adam Peterson, ... 1701

OFFICERS FOR KENT COUNTY.

Sheriffs.

Peter Bawcomb, ... 1682
Richard Michael, deceased, ...
George Martin, ... May 4, 1685–86
William Wilson, ... Feb. 20, 1704
William Rodney, ... Oct. 4, 1726

Thomas Skidmore,	Oct.	4, 1727
Moses Freeman,	Oct.	3, 1728
William Rodney,	Oct.	5, 1729
John Hall,	Oct.	3, 1730–32
Daniel Rodney,	Oct.	6, 1733–35
Samuel Robinson,	Oct.	3, 1741–42
Thomas Green,	Oct.	4, 1744–45
John Hunter,	Oct.	4, 1746
Thomas Parke,	Oct.	8, 1749–51
John Clayton, Jr.,	Oct.	4, 1752–53
Cæsar Rodney,	Oct.	4, 1755–56
Thomas Parker,	Oct.	4, 1759
Willliam Rhoades,	Oct.	3, 1760–62
Daniel Robinson,	Oct.	4, 1763
Thomas Collins,	Oct.	6, 1764–66
James Wells,	Oct.	5, 1767–69
James Caldwell,	Oct.	6, 1770–71
John Cook,	Oct.	5, 1772–74
Philip Barret,	Oct.	6, 1775

Coroners.

Thomas Stratton,	May	6, 1686
Thomas Stratton,	Mar.	15, 1690
Edward Jennings,	Oct.	4, 1726
Samuel Berry,	Oct.	4, 1727–30
Nicholas Lockerman,	Oct.	6, 1731–35
Edmund Badger,	Oct.	3, 1741–42
Thomas Parke,	Oct.	4, 1744–45
George Goforth,	Oct.	4, 1746
William Blackiston,	Oct.	8, 1749–50
James Gray,	Oct.	3, 1751
French Battell,	Oct.	4, 1752–55
Mathias Crozier,	Oct.	5, 1756
William Wells,	Oct.	4, 1757
Jabez Jenkins,	Oct.	3, 1760
John Gray,	Oct.	4, 1762–63
Matthew Manlove,	Oct.	6, 1764
John Gray,	Oct.	5, 1765
Solomon Wallace,	Oct.	4, 1766–68
Jonathan Sipple,	Oct.	6, 1769
John Smithers,	Oct.	6, 1770–71
Caleb Furbee,	Oct.	5, 1772–74
Jonathan Sipple,	Oct.	6, 1775

Recorder or Deputy Treasurer.

Richard Mitchell,	Feb.	22, 1684

56

THREE LOWER COUNTIES.

Attorney General.

John Broadshall, ...	Feb.	9, 1686

Ranger.

Simon Irons, ...	Nov.	9, 1685

Deputy Surveyor.

Benjamin Johnson, ...	Sept.	15, 1742

Clerks of the Courts.

John Brinkloe, ...		1685
William Berry, (vice Brinkloe, resigned,) . .	May	31, 1686
William Rodney, ...	May	15, 1693
William Anan, ...	Feb.	20, 1704

Justices of the Peace.

William Clarke, ...	Aug.	5, 1684
William Darnall, ...	Oct.	22, 1684
Gerardus Wessell, ...	Oct.	22, 1684
John Briggs, ...	Oct.	22, 1684
Daniel Jones, ...	Oct.	22, 1668
William Berry, ...		1684
William Southersby, ...	Jan.	9, 1685
William Frampher, ...	Jan.	9, 1685
William Berry, ...	Jan.	9, 1685
John Briggs, (resigned February 9, 1686,) . .	Jan.	9, 1685
William Winsmore, ...	Jan.	9, 1685
Thomas Hazard, ...	Jan.	9, 1685
Michael Walton, ...	Jan.	9, 1685
John Walker, ...	Jan.	9, 1685
Thomas Wilson, ...	Jan.	9, 1685
William Clarke, ...	Jan.	2, 1689
Jonathan Brinkloe, ...	Jan.	2, 1689
George Martin, ...	Jan.	2, 1689
John Curtis, ...	Jan.	2, 1689
Daniel Jones, ...	Jan.	2, 1689
John Walker, ...	Jan.	2, 1689
Mark Manlove, ...	Jan.	2, 1689
William Lawrence, ...	Jan.	2, 1689
William Freeland, ...	Jan.	2, 1689
James Brookes, ...	Jan.	2, 1689
William Manlove, ...	Jan.	2, 1689
John Brinkloe, ...	May	16, 1690
John Curtis, ...	May	16, 1690
George Martin, ...	May	16, 1690
Daniel Jones, ...	May	16, 1690
John Walker, ...	May	16, 1690
Mark Manlove, ...	May	16, 1690

William Lawrence,	May	16, 1690
William Freeland,	May	16, 1690
Thomas Rouse,	May	16, 1690
William Manlove,	May	16, 1690
Jonathan Betts,	May	16, 1690
Simon Irons,	May	16, 1690
John Brinkloe,		1693
George Martin,		1693
Daniel Jones,		1693
John Curtis,		1693
Jonathan Betts,		1693
.John Brinkloe,	Jan.	20, 1702
William Rodney,	Jan.	20, 1702
John Walker,	Jan.	20, 1702
Henry Mollesten,	Jan.	20, 1702
William Wharton,	Jan.	20, 1702
Thomas Bedwell,	Jan.	20, 1702
John Robeson,	Jan.	20, 1702
Arthur Weston,	Jan.	20, 1702
Evan Jones,	Jan.	20, 1702
George Robeson,	Jan.	20, 1702
William Winsmore,	Jan.	20, 1702
John Brinkloe,	July	10, 1710
Thomas Bedwell,	July	10, 1710
Arthur Weston,	July	10, 1710
William Winsmore,	July	10, 1710
William Brinkloe,	July	10, 1710
Evan Jones,	July	10, 1710
Charles Hilliard,	July	10, 1710
Samuel Berry,	July	10, 1710
Thomas Skidmore,	July	10, 1710
Thomas Bedwell,	Nov.	3, 1710
William Winsmore,	Nov.	3, 1710
Samuel Berry,	Nov.	3, 1710
Joseph Booth,	Nov.	3, 1710
William Brinkloe,	Nov.	3, 1710
Thomas Skidmore,	Nov.	3, 1710
John Foster,	Nov.	3, 1710
James Steel,	Nov.	3, 1710
Timothy Hanson,	Nov.	3, 1710
Samuel Berry,	May	2, 1715
Charles Hilliard,	May	2, 1715
John Forrester,	May	2, 1715
James Steel,	May	2, 1715
William Brinkloe,	May	2, 1715
Timothy Hanson,	May	2, 1715

THREE LOWER COUNTIES.

Thomas French, .	May	2, 1715
Richard Richardson,	May	2, 1715
John Coe, .	May	2, 1715
John Brinkloe,	July	10, 1717
James Steel,	July	10, 1717
Benjamin Shermer,	July	10, 1717
Robert Gordon, .	July	10, 1717
Evan Jones, .	July	10, 1717
Samuel Berry, .	July	10, 1717
William Brinckloe, .	July	10, 1717
Timothy Hanson,	July	10, 1717
Thomas French, .	July	10, 1717
Richard Richardson, .	July	10, 1717
Adam Fisher, .	July	10, 1717
Mark Manlove, .	July	10, 1717
Robert Gordon,	July	25, 1726
Benjamin Shermer,.	July	25, 1726
Richard Richardson,	July	25, 1726
Charles Hilliard, .	July	25, 1726
Thomas French,	July	25, 1726
Mark Manlove, .	July	25, 1726
Timothy Hanson, .	July	25, 1726
John Hall, .	July	25, 1726
James Worrell,	July	25, 1726
Joseph Booth, Jr.,	July	25, 1726
John Brinkloe,	July	25, 1726
Thomas Berry, .	July	25, 1726
George Newell,	July	25, 1726
John Houseman, .	July	25, 1726
John Tilton, .	July	25, 1726
William Manlove,	July	25, 1726
Hugh Durborrow, .	July	25, 1726
All Justices now acting re-commissioned,	Dec.	1, 1733
Members of Proprietary and Governor's Council,	Nov.	1, 1764
John Caton, .	Nov.	1, 1764
Richard Wells, .	Nov.	1, 1764
Thomas Irons, .	Nov.	1, 1764
Theodore Maurice, .	Nov.	1, 1764
Andrew Caldwell, .	Nov.	1, 1764
Cæsar Rodney,	Nov.	1, 1764
Charles Ridgley, .	Nov.	1, 1764
John Clarke, Jr., .	Nov.	1, 1764
John Barnes, .	Nov.	1, 1764
James Morris,	Nov.	1, 1764
James Sykes, .	Nov.	1, 1764
William Rhoades, .	Nov.	1, 1764

William Rodney,	Nov.	1, 1764
Robert Holliday,	Nov.	1, 1764
Charles Hilliard,	Nov.	1, 1764
Members of Council,	Nov.	1, 1766
John Caton,	Nov.	1, 1766
Richard Wells,	Nov.	1, 1766
Thomas Irons,	Nov.	1, 1766
Andrew Caldwell,	Nov.	1, 1766
Caesar Rodney,	Nov.	1, 1766
Charles Ridgley,	Nov.	1, 1766
Robert Killen,	Nov.	1, 1766
Jacob Stout,	Nov.	1, 1766
Fenwick Fisher,	Nov.	1, 1766
Thomas Tilton,	Nov.	1, 1766
John Barnes,	Nov.	1, 1766
James Sykes,	Nov.	1, 1766
William Rhoades,	Nov.	1, 1766
William Rodney,	Nov.	1, 1766
Robert Holliday,	Nov.	1, 1766
John Clark,	Nov.	1, 1766
Charles Ridgley,	Dec.	1, 1771
Andrew Caldwell,	Dec.	1, 1771
James Sykes,	Dec.	1, 1771
William Rhoades,	Dec.	1, 1771
John Clark,	Dec.	1, 1771
Jacob Stout,	Dec.	1, 1771
Fenwick Fisher,	Dec.	1, 1771
Thomas Tilton,	Dec.	1, 1771
Warner Mifflin,	Dec.	1, 1771
James Boyer,	Dec.	1, 1771
Thomas Hanson,	Dec.	1, 1771
Jonathan Emerson,	Dec.	1, 1771
Samuel Chew,	Dec.	1, 1771
Richard Smith,	Dec.	1, 1771
Richard Lockwood,	Dec.	1, 1771
Zadock Crapper,	Dec.	1, 1771
Members of Council,	Oct.	24, 1774
Charles Ridgley,	Oct.	24, 1774
James Sykes,	Oct.	24, 1774
William Rhoades,	Oct.	24, 1774
John Clark,	Oct.	24, 1774
Jacob Stout,	Oct.	24, 1774
Fenwick Fisher,	Oct.	24, 1774
Thomas Tilton,	Oct.	24, 1774
James Boyer,	Oct.	24, 1774
Thomas Hanson,	Oct.	24, 1774

Jonathan Emerson,	. . . . . .	Oct.	24, 1774
John Chew,	. . . .	Oct.	24, 1774
Richard Smith,	. . . .	Oct.	24, 1774
Richard Lockwood,	. . . . . .	Oct.	24, 1774
Zadock Crapper,	. . . .	Oct.	24, 1774
Thomas Rodney,	. . . .	Oct.	24, 1774
Thomas White,	. . . .	Oct.	24, 1774

Justices for Trial of Negroes.

Charles Ridgley,	. . . .	Feb.	14, 1770
Fenwick Fisher,	. . . .	Feb.	14, 1770

Dedimus Potestatems.

John Vining,	. . . .		1764
Cæsar Rodney,	. . . . . .		1764
John Vining,	. . . .	June	16, 1769
Cæsar Rodney,	. . . . . .	June	16, 1769
Cæsar Rodney,	. . . .	Oct.	24, 1774
Samuel Chew,	. . . .	Oct.	24, 1774

Trustees of the General Loan Office of Kent County.

John Vining,	. . . .	May	7, 1759
John Brinkloe,	. . . .	May	7, 1759

Signer of Bills of Credit for Kent County.

John Barns.

Assembly.

John Briggs,	1682–83
Simon Irons,	1682–83
Thomas Hazard,	1682–83
John Curtis,	1682–83
Robert Bedwell,	1682–83
William Winsmore,	1682–83
John Brinkloe,	1682–83
Daniel Brown,	1682–83
Benoni Bishop,	1682–83
John Briggs,	1684
John Glover,	1684
John Curtis,	1684
William Sherwood,	1684
James Wells,	1684
William Berry,	1684
John Bridges,	1685
John Curtis,	1685
Daniel Jones,	1685
Peter Gronendyke,	1685
William Berry,	1685

John Brinkloe, ...	1685
John Brinkloe, ...	1686
John Bradshaw, ...	1686
John Walker, ...	1686
William Berry, ...	1686
Robert Bedwell, ...	1686
Richard Wilson, ...	1686
John Brinkloe, ...	1687
William Berry, ...	1687
Richard Wilson, ...	1687
Thomas Pemberton, ...	1687
William Freeland, ...	1687
Benoni Bishop, ...	1687
John Brinkloe, ...	1688
John Betts, ...	1688
William Rodney, ...	1688
John Burton, ...	1688
Samuel Burberry, Jr., ...	1688
John Richardson, Jr., ...	1688
Daniel Jones, ...	1689
William Berry, ...	1689
William Manlove, ...	1689
John Walker, ...	1689
Peter Gronendyke, ...	1689
Daniel Brown, at New Castle, ...	1689
John Barnes, ...	1690
John Betts, ...	1690
Daniel Brown, ...	1690
Ezekiel Needham, ...	1690
Richard Curtis, ...	1690
William Freeland, ...	1690
(1691 missing.)	
William Freeland, ...	1692
Daniel Jones, ...	1692
Simon Irons, ...	1692
John Barnes, ...	1692
George Manlove, ...	1692
William Manlove, ...	1692
John Brinkloe, ...	1693
John Walker, ...	1693
William Manlove, ...	1693
John Brinkloe, ...	1694
William Freeman, ...	1694
Richard Wilson, ...	1694
John Betts, ...	1695
William Rodney, ...	1695

William Morton,	1695
Simon Irons,	1695
Daniel Brown,	1695
John Hilliard,	1695
William Rodney,	1696
William Morton,	1696
Richard Wilson,	1696
John Walker,	1697
Thomas Bedwell,	1697
Samuel Burberry,	1697
John Bradshaw,	1697
Richard Wilson,	1698
Robert Edmonds,	1698
Henry Molleston,	1698
William Morton,	1698
John Forster,	1699
Thomas Sharp,	1699
Henry Molleston,	1699
James Brown,	1699
William Morton,	1700
John Brinkloe,	1700
Richard Wilson,	1700
Griffith Jones,	1700
Arthur Weston,	1700
William Rodney,	1700
John Brinkloe, (extra session,)	1700
Richard Wilson, (extra session,)	1700
William Morton, (extra session,)	1700
Henry Molleston, (extra session,)	1700
William Rodney,	1701
John Brinkloe,	1701
William Morton,	1701
John Walker,	1701

OFFICERS FOR SUSSEX COUNTY.

Sheriffs.

John Vines,		1682
John Hill,	Nov.	9, 1685
Francis Conwell,		1687
William Rodney,	Dec.	1688
Samuel Preston,	May	30, 1690
John Hill,	April	28, 1693

Jonathan Bailey,		
Luke Watson, Sen.,	June	24, 1703–04
Ryves Holt,	Oct.	4, 1726–29
Simon Kollock,	Oct.	3, 1730–33
Cornelius Wiltbank,	Oct.	5, 1734
John Shankland,	Oct.	5, 1735
Peter Hall,	Oct.	3, 1741–42
William Shankland,	Oct.	4, 1744–46
Peter Clowes,	Oct.	8, 1749
William Shankland,	Oct.	6, 1750–52
Jacob Kollock, Jr.,	Oct.	4, 1753–55
John Rodney,	Oct.	5, 1756
Joseph Shankland,	Oct.	4, 1759–60
Daniel Nunez, Jr.,	Oct.	4, 1762–64
Rhoads Shankland,	Oct.	5, 1765–67
Boaz Manlove,	Oct.	6, 1768–70
Peter Robinson,	Oct.	7, 1771–72
Thos Robinson,	Oct.	19, 1773
Dorman Lofland,	Oct.	5, 1774–75

Coroners.

John Vines,	Feb.	9, 1686
Samuel Davis,	Oct.	4, 1726–27
John Jacobs,	Oct.	3, 1728
John Rhoades,	Oct.	5, 1729
Cornelius Wiltbank,	Oct.	3, 1730
John Clowes,	Oct.	6, 1731
Joshua Fisher,	Oct.	5, 1732–34
Daniel Nunez,	Oct.	5, 1735
Peter Clowes,	Oct.	3, 1741–42
Robert Gill,	Oct.	4, 1744–45
John Molleston,	Oct.	4, 1746
William Shankland,	Oct.	8, 1749
Robert McIlwaine,	Oct.	6, 1750
John Rodney,	Oct.	3, 1751–52
John Spencer,	Oct.	3, 1753
Paynter Stockley,	Oct.	4, 1755
Wrixham Lewis,	Oct.	5, 1756
Jabez Maud Fisher,	Oct.	4, 1759
David Shankland,	Oct.	3, 1760
Samuel Rowland, Jr.,	Oct.	4, 1762
John Walton,	Oct.	4, 1763
Henry Davis,	Oct.	6, 1764
Nathan Young,	Oct.	5, 1765
Thomas Gray,	Oct.	4, 1766
William Parker,	Oct.	5, 1767

George Walker,	Oct.	6, 1768
William Chance,	Oct.	6, 1769
Reese Wolfe,	Oct.	6, 1770
Eli Parker,	Oct.	7, 1771
David Train,	Oct.	6, 1772
John Draper,	Oct.	19, 1773
Lyttleton Townsend,	Oct.	5, 1774
Samuel Draper,	Oct.	12, 1775

Collector of Customs at Lewes, formerly Whorekills.

Richard Medcalf.		
Peter Razer, (vice Medcalf, deceased,)	June 28,	1760–62
David Hall,	May 16,	1763
Peter Razer.		
Daniel Nunez, Jr., (vice Razer, deceased,)	Dec. 15,	1766
Jacob Kollock,	Sept. 23,	1767

Comptroller of Customs at Lewes.

Robert Greenall,	Oct.	15, 1764

Trustees of the General Loan Office of Sussex County.

Jacob Kollock,	May	7, 1759
Ryves Holt,	May	7, 1759
Jacob Kollock,		1764
John Rodney,		1764
Jacob Kollock,	June	16, 1769
John Rodney,	June	16, 1769
David Hall, (vice Kollock, deceased,)	June	13, 1772

Signer of Bills of Credit for Sussex County.

David Hall,	May	7, 1759

Judges of the Orphans' Court.

John Hill,		
James Walker, } Court held	Nov.	6, 1782
Philip Russell,		

Attorney General.

Joshua Barkstead,	Feb.	9, 1686

Clerk.

Nehemiah Field,	May 8,	1693–1704

Prothonotary or Clerk of Common Pleas.

Jacob Kollock, Jr.,	May	16, 1763

Clerk of Orphans' Court or Register of Wills.

Jacob Kollock, resigned.		
Phillips Kollock,	Nov.	8, 1770

Clerk of the Peace and Quarter Sessions of Peace.

Norton Claypoole, ...	May	12, 1683
David Hall, ...	May	16, 1763

Deputy Surveyor.

William Shankland, ...	April	9, 1735

Rangers.

Henry Bowman, ...	May	9, 1685
John Rhoads, ...	March	16, 1687

Justices of the Peace.

John Kipshaven, ...		1681
John Rhoades, ...		1681
Edward Southern, ...		1682
William Clark, ...	May	1, 1683
Alexander Molleston, ...	May	3, 1683
Hercules Shepherd, ...		1683
Thomas Hart, ...		1683
Robert Hart, ...	Mar.	11, 168¾
Alexander Draper, ...	Mar.	11, 168¾
Robert Brassey, ...	Mar.	11, 168¾
Francis Conwell, (suspended 1686.)		
William Clarke, ...	June	5, 1686
John Rhoades, ...	June	5, 1686
Thomas Langhorne, ...	June	5, 1686
Thomas Price, ...	June	5, 1686
Robert Clifton, ...	June	5, 1686
Samuel Gray, ...	June	5, 1686
George Young, ...	June	5, 1686
William Clarke, ...	Jan.	2, 1689
Thomas Wynne, ...	Jan.	2, 1689
Luke Watson, ...	Jan.	2, 1689
John Hill, ...	Jan.	2, 1689
Thomas Price, ...	Jan.	2, 1689
Samuel Preston, ...	Jan.	2, 1689
Robert Clifton, ...	Jan.	2, 1689
Samuel Gray, ...	Jan.	2, 1689
William Clarke, ...	May	2, 1693
Luke Watson, ...	May	2, 1693

Albert Jacobs, Robert Clifton, John Stokely, Thomas Oldman, } at a Court held . . .	Mar.	6, 1693
Samuel Gray, Joseph Booth, } at a Court held . . .	June	6, 1694
Thomas Pemberton, at a Court held . .	Aug.	7, 1694

William Clarke,	Aug.	16, 1702
John Hill,	Aug.	16, 1702
Luke Watson, Jr.,	Aug.	16, 1702
Thomas Pemberton,	Aug.	16, 1702
Thomas Fenwich,	Aug.	16, 1702
James Walker,	Aug.	16, 1702
Philip Russell,	Aug.	16, 1702
John Hill,	May	3, 1706
Thomas Fisher,	May	3, 1706
Luke Waln,	May	3, 1706
Joseph Booth,	May	3, 1706
Jonathan Bayley,	May	3, 1706
James Walker,	May	3, 1706
Philip Russell,	May	3, 1706
John Waltham,	May	3, 1706
William Bagwell,	May	3, 1706
Thomas Fisher,	Dec.	14, 1708
Jonathan Bayley,	Dec.	14, 1708
James Walker,	Dec.	14, 1708
Philip Russell,	Dec.	14, 1708
William Bagwell,	Dec.	14, 1708
Cornelius Wiltbank,	Dec.	14, 1708
Richard Paynter,	Dec.	14, 1708
Samuel Watson,	Dec.	14, 1708
James Sutton,	Dec.	14, 1708
Jonathan Bayley,	Nov.	10, 1715
Barclay Codd,	Nov.	10, 1715
James Sutton,	Nov.	10, 1715
Henry Brooke,	July	25, 1726
William Till,	July	25, 1726
Philip Russell,	July	25, 1726
Samuel Rowland,	July	25, 1726
Woolsey Burton,	July	25, 1726
Simon Kollock,	July	25, 1726
John May,	July	25, 1726
Jeremiah Claypoole,	July	25, 1726
Jacob Kollock,	July	25, 1726
Thomas Davis,	July	25, 1726
John Jacobs,	July	25, 1726
Samuel Davis,	July	25, 1726
Joseph Cord,	July	25, 1726
Henry Brooke,	Sept.	23, 1726
Richard Hinman,	Sept.	23, 1726
Philip Russell,	Sept.	23, 1726
John Rhoades,	Sept.	23, 1726
Woolsey Burton,	Sept.	23, 1726

Samuel Rowland,	Sept.	23, 1726
Jeremiah Claypoole,	Sept.	23, 1726
Jacob Kollock,	Sept.	23, 1726
John Jacobs,	Sept.	23, 1726
Samuel Davis,	Sept.	23, 1726
Joseph Cord,	Sept.	23, 1726
Robert Shankland,	Sept.	23, 1726
George Walton,	Sept.	23, 1726
Enoch Cumings,	Sept.	23, 1726
David Smith,	Sept.	23, 1726
James James,	Sept.	1, 1727
All Justices now acting re-commissioned	Dec.	1, 1733
Members of Proprietary and Governor's Council,	Nov.	1, 1764
Jacob Kollock, Sr.,	Nov.	1, 1764
Benjamin Stockley,	Nov.	1, 1764
David Hall,	Nov.	1, 1764
Benjamin Burton,	Nov.	1, 1764
Nehemiah Draper,	Nov.	1, 1764
Thomas Prettyman,	Nov.	1, 1764
Jacob Kollock, Jr.,	Nov.	1, 1764
John Spencer,	Nov.	1, 1764
Isaac Watson,	Nov.	1, 1764
Wrixham Lewis,	Nov.	1, 1764
Gilbercher Parker,	Nov.	1, 1764
Levin Crapper,	Nov.	1, 1764
Tho⁹ Robinson,	Nov.	1, 1764
John Rodney,	March	20, 1767
Anderson Parker,	March	20, 1767
Cornelius Turner,	March	20, 1767
Parker Robinson,	March	20, 1767
Boaz Manlove,	March	20, 1767
John Wiltbank,	March	20, 1767
Benjamin Burton,	April	10, 1773
Jacob Kollock,	April	10, 1773
Wrixham Lewis,	April	10, 1773
Gilbercher Parker,	April	10, 1773
Levin Crapper,	April	10, 1773
Thomas Robinson,	April	10, 1773
William Conwell,	April	10, 1773
John Rodney,	April	10, 1773
Anderson Parker,	April	10, 1773
Parker Robinson,	April	10, 1773
Boaz Manlove,	April	10, 1773
John Wiltbank,	April	10, 1773
Daniel Nunez,	April	10, 1773
Nehemiah Davis,	April	10, 1773

Members of Council,	. . . . . .	Oct.	24, 1774
Benjamin Burton,	. . . . . .	Oct.	24, 1774
Jacob Kollock,	. . . .	Oct.	24, 1774
Wrixham Lewis,	. . . .	Oct.	24, 1774
Gilbercher Parker,	. . . .	Oct.	24, 1774
Levin Crapper,	. . . .	Oct.	24, 1774
Thomas Robinson,	. . . .	Oct.	24, 1774
William Conwell,	. . . . . .	Oct.	24, 1774
Boaz Manlove,	. . . .	Oct.	24, 1774
John Wiltbank,	. . . .	Oct.	24, 1774
Daniel Nunez,	. . . .	Oct.	24, 1774
Nehemiah Davis,	. . . . . .	Oct.	24, 1774
John Dagworthy,	. . . .	Oct.	24, 1774
William Holland,	. . . . . .	Oct.	24, 1774
William Elligood,	. . . .	Oct.	24, 1774
John Rodney,	. . . .	Oct.	24, 1774
Anderson Parker,	. . . .	Oct.	24, 1774
Parker Robinson,	. . . . . .	Oct.	24, 1774
William Polk,	. . . .	Oct.	24, 1774
Jonathan Bell,	. . . .	Oct.	24, 1774
Job Ingram,	. . . .	Sept.	2, 1775
Joshua Hill,	. . . .	Sept.	2, 1775
John Law,	. . . .	Sept.	2, 1775
Isaac Horsey,	. . . .	Sept.	2, 1775
Jeremiah Cannon,	. . . .	Sept.	2, 1775
Daniel Dingee,	. . . .	Sept.	2, 1775
Luke Shield, Jr.,	. . . .	Sept.	2, 1775

Dedimus Potestatems to

David Hall,	. . . .	April	10, 1773
Jacob Kollock, Jr.,	. . . .	April	10, 1773
David Hall,	. . . .	Oct.	24, 1774
John Rodney,	. . . .	Oct.	24, 1774

Assembly.

Luke Watson,	. . . .	1682–83
Alexander Draper,	. . . .	1682–83
William Fisher,	. . . .	1682–83
Henry Bowman,	. . . .	1682–83
Alexander Molleston,	. . . . . .	1682–83
John Hill,	. . . .	1682–83
Robert Brassey,	. . . .	1682–83
John Kipshaven,	. . . .	1682–83
Cornelius Verhoof,	. . . . . .	1682–83
John Rhoades,	. . . .	1684
Henry Bowman,	. . . .	1684
Hercules Shepherd,	. . . .	1684

Samuel Gray,	1684
William Emmet,	1684
Henry Stretcher,	1684
Henry Smith,	1685
William Carter,	1685
Robert Clifton,	1685
John Hill,	1685
Samuel Gray,	1685
Richard Law,	1685
Henry Bowman,	1686
Norton Claypoole,	1686
Henry Stretcher,	1686
John Vines,	1686
Albertus Jacobs,	1686
Samuel Gray,	1686
Luke Watson,	1687
Henry Smith,	1687
Henry Molleston,	1687
Henry Bowman,	1687
Samuel Gray,	1687
Henry Stretcher,	1687
Thomas Wayne,	1688
Henry Bowman,	1688
Henry Molleston,	1688
Thomas Price,	1688
John Symons,	1688
Albertus Jacobs,	1688
Baptist Newcombe,	1689
Samuel Gray,	1689
Robert Clifton,	1689
Henry Sheppard,	1689
Luke Watson, Jr.,	1689
Jonathan Bailey, at New Castle,	1689
John Hill,	1690
Samuel Gray,	1690
Robert Clifton,	1690
Henry Smith,	1690
Baptist Newcombe,	1690
Thomas Branson,	1690
William Clarke, (Speaker,)	1692
Robert Clifton,	1692
Baptist Newcombe,	1692
Luke Watson, Jr.,	1692
Thomas Branson,	1692
William Piles,	1692
Albertus Jacobs,	1693

Thomas Pemberton,	1693
Samuel Preston,	1693
Thomas Pemberton,	1694
Luke Watson,	1694
Roger Corbit,	1694
John Stockley,	1695
Thomas Oldman,	1695
Joseph Booth,	1695
Henry Molleston,	1695
James Peterkill,	1695
Jonathan Bailey,	1695
Thomas Pemberton,	1696
Roger Corbit,	1696
John Miers,	1696
Luke Watson,	1697
Thomas Oldman,	1697
Nehemiah Field,	1697
Thomas Fisher,	1697
Thomas Oldman,	1698
Jonathan Bailey,	1698
Luke Watson, Jr.,	1698
Cornelius Wiltbank,	1698
William Piles,	1699
William Fisher,	1699
Nehemiah Field,	1699
William Dyer,	1690
Joseph Booth,	1700
Thomas Pemberton,	1700
Luke Watson, Jr.,	1700
Thomas Fisher,	1700
Arthur Vankirk,	1700
Robert Burton,	1700
John Hill, (extra session,)	1700
Thomas Pemberton, (extra session,)	1700
Luke Watson, Jr., (extra session,)	1700
Thomas Fenwick, (extra session,)	1700
William Clarke,	1701
Luke Watson, Jr.,	1701
Samuel Preston,	1701
Joseph Booth,	1701

71

PROVINCIAL OFFICERS

FOR THE

THREE ORIGINAL COUNTIES,

CHESTER, PHILADELPHIA, AND BUCKS.

1682—1776.

CHESTER, PHILADELPHIA, AND BUCKS.

OFFICERS FOR CHESTER COUNTY.

Sheriffs.

John Test,	1681
Thomas Usher,	1682-86
Joseph Wood,	April 28, 1693
Andrew Job,	Mar. 31, 1701
John Hoskins,	Oct. 15, 1703-10
Nicholas Fairlamb,	Oct. 3, 1717-19
John Crosby,	Oct. 4, 1720
John Taylor,	Oct. 4, 1721-28
John Owen,	Oct. 4, 1729-31
John Parry,	Oct. 3, 1732-34
John Owen,	Oct. 3, 1735-37
John Parry,	Oct. 4, 1738-39
Benjamin Davis,	Oct. 3, 1740-42
John Owen,	Oct. 4, 1743-45
Benjamin Davis,	Oct. 4, 1746-48
John Owen,	Oct. 8, 1749-51
Isaac Pearson,	Oct. 4, 1752-54
John Fairlamb,	Oct. 4, 1755-56
Benjamin Davis,	Oct. 4, 1759-60
John Fairlamb,	Oct. 4, 1762-63
Philip Ford,	Oct. 4, 1764-66
John Morton, (vice Philip Ford, deceased,)	Oct. 28, 1766-68
Jesse Maris,	Oct. 5, 1769-71
Henry Hayes,	Oct. 5, 1772-73
Nathaniel Vernon,	Oct. 5, 1774-75

Coroners.

James Kennerly,	1685
Jacob Symcock,	1691
James Sandelands,	Oct. 3, 1717-20
Robert Barber,	Oct. 4, 1721
John Mendenhall,	Oct. 4, 1726-27
Robert Parke,	Oct. 3, 1728
Abraham Darlington,	Oct. 4, 1729
John Wharton,	Oct. 3, 1730-31

75

Anthony Shaw, ... Oct. 3, 1732–33
John Wharton, ... Oct. 4, 1734–36
Stephen Hoskins, ... Oct. 4, 1737
Aubrey Bevan, ... Oct. 4, 1738–42
Thomas Morgan, ... Oct. 4, 1743–45
Isaac Lea, ... Oct. 4, 1746–50
Joshua Thomson, ... Oct. 3, 1751
John Kerlin, ... Oct. 4, 1752
Joshua Thomson, ... Oct. 3, 1753–62
Philip Ford, (vice Thomson, deceased, . . May 22, 1761–62
Davis Bevan, ... Oct. 4, 1763–64
Abel Janney, ... Oct. 4, 1765
John Trapnall, (vice Janney, resigned,) . . May 27, 1766
Joseph Gibbons, Jr., ... Oct. 4, 1768–70
John Crosby, Jr., ... Oct. 5, 1771–72
John Bryan, ... Oct. 4, 1773–76

Collectors of Excise.

Caleb Cowpland, ... 1731–33
John Owen, ... 1733–37
Thomas Cummings, ... 1738–43
Jeremiah Starr, ... 1744–56
Charles Humphreys, ... 1757–73
Thomas Tucker, ... 1773–76

Treasurers.

Caleb Pusey, ... 1704
Philip Taylor, ... 1724–26
Robert Miller, ... 1757–59
Humphrey Marshall, ... 1762–65
Lewis Davis, ... 1766–69
James Gibbons, ... 1770–75
Philip Taylor, ... 1775

Receiver or Deputy Treasurer.

Thomas Usher, ... Feb. 22, 1684

Collectors of Money granted Proprietor.

Andrew Job, ... March 28, 1704
John Hoskins, ... March 28, 1704
Henry Hollingsworth, ... March 28, 1704

Deputy Surveyor.

Charles Ashcomb, ... 1665

Prothonotary.

Robert Assheton, ... 1712

Clerk of Peace and Prothonotary.

Joseph Parker, ... Feb. 16, 1733–34

Prothonotary, Clerk of Courts and Recorder.

Henry Hale Graham, ... 1770–77

Sealer of Weights and Measures.

Isaac Taylor, ... Dec. 22, 1741

Flour Inspector.

Thomas Cummings, ... 1750

Recorder.

Henry Hale Graham, ... 1773–75

Late Constable and Collector in Sadbury Township.

David McClure, ... 1770

Justices for the Trial of Negroes.

William Parker, ... Jan. 22. 1770
Richard Riley, ... Jan. 22, 1770
John Morton, ... Dec. 24, 1770
William Parker, ... Dec. 24, 1770

Justices of the Peace.

John Simcock, ... 1683
Thomas Brassey, ... 1683
John Bezer, ... 1683
Ralph Withers, ... 1683
Christopher Taylor, ... 1684
William Wood, ... 1684
Nicholas Newlin, ... 1684
George Maris, ... 1684
Thomas Usher, ... 1684
Robert Pyle, ... 1684
John Blunston, ... 1684
John Harding, ... 1684
John Simcock, ... April 6, 1685
William Wood, ... April 6, 1685
Nicholas Newlin, ... April 6, 1685
Robert Wade, ... April 6, 1685
George Maris, ... April 6. 1685
Thomas Usher, ... April 6, 1685
Robert Pyle, ... April 6, 1685
John Blunston, ... April 6, 1685
Bartholomew Coppock, ... 1686
Samuel Levis, ... 1686
Francis Harrison, ... 1686

77

John Bristow,		1687
Edward Bezar,		1687
Bartholomew Coppock, Jr.,		1688
John Bristow,	Nov.	2, 1689
John Bevan,	Nov.	2, 1689
John Blunston,	Nov.	2, 1689
Nicholas Newlin,	Nov.	2, 1689
Francis Harrison,	Nov.	2, 1689
Samuel Levis,	Nov.	2, 1689
James Sandelands,	Nov.	2, 1689
William Howell,	Nov.	2, 1689
Josiah Fearn,	Nov.	2, 1689
William Jenkins,		1691
John Simcock,		1692
John Bristow,		1692
George Maris,		1692
William Jenkins,		1692
Jonathan Hayes,		1692
Robert Pyle,		1692
Randall Vernon,		1692
George Forman,	May	13, 1693
John Child,	May	13, 1693
John Blunston,	June	19, 1684
Thomas Usher,	June	19, 1684
George Maris,	June	19, 1684
Jeremiah Collett,	May	13, 1693
Thomas Smith,	May	13, 1693
Thomas Withers,	May	13, 1693
Peter Baynton,	May	13, 1693
Jonathan Hayes,	May	13, 1693
Jasper Yeates,		1694
Philip Roman,		1698
Caleb Pusey,		1698
Ralph Fishbourne,		1700
Walter Martin,		1702
John Guest,	Sept.	25, 1703
Jasper Yeates,	Sept.	25, 1703
Caleb Pusey,	Sept.	25, 1703
Philip Roman,	Sept.	25, 1703
Jonathan Hayes,	Sept.	25, 1703
Ralph Fishbourne,	Sept.	25, 1703
Jeremiah Collett,	Sept.	25, 1703
Walter Martin,	Sept.	25, 1703
Nathaniel Newlin,	Sept.	25, 1703
James Powell,		1709
Henry Pierce,		1709

Nicholas Pyle,		1709
William Davis,	Oct.	16, 1712
Caleb Pusey,	May	30, 1715
Nicholas Pyle,	May	30, 1715
Richard Webb,	May	30, 1715
Henry Pierce,	May	30, 1715
Henry Nayle,	May	30, 1715
Nicholas Fairlamb,	May	30, 1715
John Blunston, Jr.,	May	30, 1715
Richard Hayes,	May	30, 1715
John Wright,		1717
David Harry,		1717
Joseph Coburn,		1717
Henry Hayes,		1717
John Wright,	July	4, 1718
Andrew Job,	July	4, 1718
John Cartlidge,	July	4, 1718
Nathaniel Newlin,	July	4, 1718
Elisha Gatchell,	July	4, 1718
Francis Worley,	July	4, 1718
James Gibbons,	July	4, 1718
Francis Worley,	May	28, 1722
James Mitchell,	July	24, 1722
Isaac Taylor,	Nov.	5, 1722
Elisha Gatchell,	Nov.	5, 1722
James Mitchell,	April	25, 1723
John Wood,		1724
Samuel Nutt,		1724
John Crosby,		1724
Abraham Emmett, Jr.,		1724
Thomas Reid,		1724
George Ashton,		1724
Tobias Hendricks,		1724
Andrew Cornish,		1724
Mercer Brown,		1724
Evan Lewis,		1724
William Pyle,		1724
John Wright,	Aug.	25, 1726
Richard Hayes,	Aug.	25, 1726
Henry Pierce,	Aug.	25, 1726
Nathaniel Newlin,	Aug.	25, 1726
John Wood,	Aug.	25, 1726
Henry Hayes,	Aug.	25, 1726
Isaac Taylor,	Aug.	25, 1726
Elisha Gatchell,	Aug.	25, 1726
Samuel Nutt,	Aug.	25, 1726

John Crosby,	Aug.	25, 1726
Abraham Emmet, Jr.,	Aug.	25, 1726
Thomas Reid,	Aug.	25, 1726
George Aston,	Aug.	25, 1726
Tobias Hendricks,	Aug.	25, 1726
Andrew Cornish,	Aug.	25, 1726
Mercer Brown,	Aug.	25, 1726
Evan Lewis,	Aug.	25, 1726
William Pyle,	Aug.	25, 1726
Richard Hayes,	Feb.	19, 1729-30
Henry Pierce,	Feb.	19, 1729-30
Henry Hayes,	Feb.	19, 1729-30
Elisha Gatchell,	Feb.	19, 1729-30
John Crosby,	Feb.	19, 1729-30
Abraham Emmett, Jr.,	Feb.	19, 1729-30
Mercer Brown,	Feb.	19, 1729-30
James James,	Feb.	19, 1729-30
John Parry,	Feb.	19, 1729-30
James Gibbons,	Feb.	19, 1729-30
Joseph Pennock,	Feb.	19, 1729-30
Samuel Hollingsworth,	Feb.	19, 1729-30
Joseph Brinton,	Feb.	19, 1729-30
Nicholas Pyle,	Feb.	19, 1729-30
The Chief Burgess of the borough of Chester,	Feb.	19, 1729-30
John Karnaghan,		1731
All Justices now acting re-commissioned,	Dec.	1, 1733
Caleb Cowpland,	Dec.	1, 1733
Joseph Haines,	May	25, 1734
John Evans,	Dec.	2, 1737
Richard Hayes,	Nov.	22, 1738
Henry Pierce,	Nov.	22, 1738
Henry Hayes,	Nov.	22, 1738
Elisha Gatchell,	Nov.	22, 1738
John Crosby,	Nov.	22, 1738
Caleb Cowpland,	Nov.	22, 1738
Abraham Emmett,	Nov.	22, 1738
James James,	Nov.	22, 1738
John Parry,	Nov.	22, 1738
Joseph Pennock,	Nov.	22, 1738
Samuel Hollingsworth,	Nov.	22, 1738
Joseph Brinton,	Nov.	22, 1738
Joseph Haines,	Nov.	22, 1738
William Pim,	Nov.	22, 1738
Joseph Bonsall,	Nov.	22, 1738
The Chief Burgess of the town for the time being,	Nov.	22, 1738
Joseph Parker,	Nov.	22, 1738

Henry Pierce,	April	4, 1741
Henry Hayes,	April	4, 1741
Elisha Gatchell,	April	4, 1741
John Crosby,	April	4, 1741
Caleb Cowpland,	April	4, 1741
William Moore, Presiding Justice,	April	4, 1741
Abraham Emmett,	April	4, 1741
Joseph Pennock,	April	4, 1741
Joseph Brinton,	April	4. 1741
William Pim,	April	4, 1741
Joseph Bonsall,	April	4, 1741
Joseph Parker,	April	4, 1741
William Webb,	April	4, 1741
John Mather,	April	4, 1741
Ralph Pyle,	April	4, 1741
John Taylor,	April	4, 1741
Job Ruston,	April	4, 1741
Charles Grantham,	April	4, 1741
The Chief Burgess of Chester,	April	4, 1741
John Crosby,	Dec.	17, 1745
Elisha Gatchell,	Dec.	17, 1745
Caleb Cowpland,	Dec.	17, 1745
William Moore,	Dec.	17, 1745
Abraham Emmett,	Dec.	17, 1745
Joseph Pennock,	Dec.	17, 1745
Joseph Brinton,	Dec.	17, 1745
William Pim,	Dec.	17, 1745
Joseph Bonsall,	Dec.	17, 1745
William Webb,	Dec.	17, 1745
John Mather,	Dec.	17, 1745
Job Ruston,	Dec.	17, 1745
Charles Grantham,	Dec.	17, 1745
Samuel Flower,	Dec.	17, 1745
Thomas Cummings,	Dec.	17, 1745
John Parry,	Dec.	17, 1745
Andrew McDowell,	Dec.	17, 1745
The Chief Burgess of Chester for the time being,	Dec.	17, 1745
Joseph Parker, (separate Com.,)	Dec.	17, 1745
Caleb Cowpland,	May	19, 1749
Elisha Gatchell,	May	19, 1749
William Moore,	May	19, 1749
Joseph Pennock,	May	19, 1749
Joseph Brinton,	May	19, 1749
William Pim,	May	19, 1749
Joseph Bonsall,	May	19, 1749
John Mather,	May	19, 1749

Charles Grantham,	May	19, 1749
Samuel Flower,	May	19, 1749
Thomas Cummings,	May	19, 1749
Thomas Worth,	May	19, 1749
Aaron Ashbridge,	May	19, 1749
John Churchman,	May	19, 1749
John Miller,	May	19, 1749
Richard Richardson,	May	19, 1749
Isaac Davis,	May	19, 1749
John Scott,	May	19, 1749
William Read,	May	19, 1749
The Chief Burgess of Chester for the time being,	May	19, 1749
Joshua Pusey,		1751
Samuel Lightfoot,		1751
William Moore,	May	25, 1752
Elisha Gatchell,	May	25, 1752
Joseph Bonsall,	May	25, 1752
John Mather,	May	25, 1752
Charles Grantham,	May	25, 1752
Samuel Flower,	May	25, 1752
Thomas Cummings,	May	25, 1752
Thomas Worth,	May	25, 1752
Aaron Ashbridge,	May	25, 1752
John Churchman,	May	25, 1752
John Miller,	May	25, 1752
Isaac Davis,	May	25, 1752
John Scott,	May	25, 1752
Joshua Pusey,	May	25, 1752
Samuel Lightfoot,	May	25, 1752
Edward Brinton,	May	25, 1752
Mordecai Moore,	May	25, 1752
Mordecai James,	May	25, 1752
The Chief Burgess of Chester for the time being,	May	25, 1752
William Moore,	Feb.	22, 1757
John Mather,	Feb.	22, 1757
Samuel Flower,	Feb.	22, 1757
Thomas Worth,	Feb.	22, 1757
Aaron Ashbridge,	Feb.	22, 1757
John Miller,	Feb.	22, 1757
Isaac Davis,	Feb.	22, 1757
John Scott,	Feb.	22, 1757
Samuel Lightfoot,	Feb.	22, 1757
Edward Brinton,	Feb.	22, 1757
Mordecai Moore,	Feb.	22, 1757
The Chief Burgess of Chester,	Feb.	22, 1757
Alexander Johnston,	Feb.	22, 1757

John Morton, ...	Feb.	22, 1757
John Culbertson, ...	Feb.	22, 1757
William Clingan, ...	Feb.	22, 1757
John Paschall, ...	Feb.	22, 1757
William Parker, ...	Feb.	22, 1757
Timothy Kirk, ...	Feb.	22, 1757
Thomas Worth, ...	Feb.	23, 1761
Samuel Flower, ...	Feb.	23, 1761
John Miller, ...	Feb.	23, 1761
Isaac Davis, ...	Feb.	23, 1761
Edward Brinton, ...	Feb.	23, 1761
The Chief Burgess of Chester, ...	Feb.	23, 1761
Alexander Johnston, ...	Feb.	23, 1761
John Morton, ...	Feb.	23, 1761
John Culbertson, ...	Feb.	23, 1761
William Clingan, ...	Feb.	23, 1761
William Parker, ...	Feb.	23, 1761
Timothy Kirk, ...	Feb.	23, 1761
John Hannum, ...	Feb.	23, 1761
John Price, ...	Feb.	23, 1761
Roger Hunt, ...	Feb.	23, 1761
John Fairlamb, ...	Feb.	23, 1761
George Currie, ...	Feb.	23, 1761
Henry Hale Graham, ...	Feb.	23, 1761
Members of Council, ...	Nov.	19, 1764
William Moore, ...	Nov.	19, 1764
Thomas Worth, ...	Nov.	19, 1764
Samuel Flower, ...	Nov.	19, 1764
John Miller, ...	Nov.	19, 1764
Isaac Davis, ...	Nov.	19, 1764
Edward Brinton, ...	Nov.	19, 1764
Alexander Johnston, ...	Nov.	19, 1764
John Culbertson, ...	Nov.	19, 1764
William Clingan, ...	Nov.	19, 1764
William Parker, ...	Nov.	19, 1764
John Hannum, ...	Nov.	19, 1764
John Price, ...	Nov.	19, 1764
John Fairlamb, ...	Nov.	19, 1764
Henry Hale Graham, ...	Nov.	19, 1764
William Boyd, ...	Nov.	19, 1764
Richard Riley, ...	Nov.	19, 1764
James Hunter, ...	Nov.	19, 1764
James Evans, ...	Nov.	19, 1764
Members of Council, ...	May	23, 1770
William Moore, ...	May	23, 1770
Thomas Worth, ...	May	23, 1770

John Morton,	May	23, 1770
Isaac Davis,	May	23, 1770
Alexander Johnston,	May	23, 1770
William Clingan,	May	23, 1770
William Parker,	May	23, 1770
John Hannum,	May	23, 1770
John Price,	May	23, 1770
Henry Hale Graham,	May	23, 1770
Richard Riley,	May	23, 1770
Charles Cruikshanks,	May	23, 1770
Richard Baker,	May	23, 1770
James Gibbons,	May	23, 1770
James Moore,	May	23, 1770
William Swaffer,	May	23, 1770
Evan Evans,	May	23, 1770
Thomas Hockley,	May	23, 1770
Joseph Pyle,	May	23, 1770
Thomas Temple,	May	23, 1770
Warwick Miller,	May	23, 1770
Joshua Cowpland,		1772
William Moore,		1775

Assembly.

John Hoskins,	1682–3
Robert Wade,	1682–3
George Wood,	1682–3
John Blunston,	1682–3
Dennis Rochford,	1682–3
Thomas Brassey,	1682–3
John Bezar,	1682–3
John Harding,	1682–3
Joseph Phipps,	1682–3
Joshua Hastings,	1684
Robert Wade,	1684
John Blunston,	1684
George Maris,	1684
Thomas Usher,	1684
Henry Maddock,	1684
John Blunston,	1685
George Maris,	1685
John Harding,	1685
Thomas Usher,	1685
Francis Stanfield,	1685
Josiah Fearn,	1685
Robert Wade,	1686
John Blunston,	1686

George Maris,	1686
Bartholomew Coppock,	1686
Samuel Lewis,	1686
Caleb Pusey,	1686
John Blunston,	1687
George Maris,	1687
Bartholomew Coppock,	1687
Caleb Pusey,	1687
Edward Bezar,	1687
Randall Vernon,	1687
John Blunston,	1688
James Sandelands,	1688
George Maris,	1688
Robert Pyle,	1688
Edward Carter,	1688
Thomas Coeburn,	1688
James Sandelands,	1689
Samuel Levis,	1689
John Bartram,	1689
Robert Pyle,	1689
Michael Blunston,	1689
Jonathan Hayes,	1689
John Bristow,	1690
William Jenkins,	1690
Robert Pyle,	1690
Josiah Fearn,	1690
George Maris,	1690
Caleb Pusey,	1690
Philip Roman,	1692
George Maris,	1692
Bartholomew Coppock,	1692
Robert Pyle,	1692
Caleb Pusey,	1692
Thomas Withers,	1692
John Simcock,	1693
George Maris,	1693
David Lloyd,	1693
David Lloyd, Speaker,	1694
Caleb Pusey,	1694
Samuel Levis,	1694
John Blunston,	1695
Bartholomew Coppock,	1695
William Jenkins,	1695
Robert Pyle,	1695
Walter Forest,	1695
Philip Roman,	1695

85

John Simcock, Speaker,	1696
John Blunston,	1696
Caleb Pusey,	1696
John Blunston, Speaker,	1697
Bartholomew Coppock,	1697
Thomas Worth,	1697
Jonathan Hayes,	1697
Caleb Pusey,	1698
Samuel Levis,	1698
Nathaniel Newlin,	1698
Robert Carter,	1698
John Blunston, Speaker,	1699
Robert Pyle,	1699
John Worrilow,	1699
Robert Carter,	1699
John Blunston, Speaker,	1700
Robert Pyle,	1700
Richard Ormes,	1700
John Hood,	1700
Samuel Levis,	1700
Henry Lewis,	1700
Joseph Baker, (extra session.)	1700
Samuel Levis, (extra session,)	1700
Nathaniel Newlin, (extra session,)	1700
Nicholas Pyle, (extra session,)	1700
John Blunston,	1701
Robert Pyle,	1701
Nathaniel Newlin,	1701
Andrew Job,	1701
Nicholas Pyle,	1704
John Bennett,	1704
Nicholas Fairlamb,	1704
Joseph Coeburn,	1704
John Hood,	1704
Richard Hayes,	1704
Joseph Wood,	1704
Isaac Taylor,	1704
Robert Pyle,	1705
Richard Webb,	1705
Caleb Pusey,	1705
Nicholas Fairlamb,	1705
John Bennett,	1705
Isaac Taylor,	1705
Nathaniel Newlin,	1705
Joseph Coeburn,	1705
Samuel Levis,	1706

Richard Hayes, ... 1706
Francis Chadds, ... 1706
Joseph Baker, ... 1706
Evan Lewis, ... 1706
John Hood, ... 1706
George Pearce, ... 1706
William Garrett, ... 1706
Francis Chadds, ... 1707
William Smith, ... 1707
Samuel Levis, ... 1707
Richard Hayes, ... 1707
John Hood, ... 1707
William Garrett, ... 1707
John Bethell, ... 1707
Evan Lewis, ... 1707
Daniel Williamson, ... 1708
Samuel Levis, ... 1708
Henry Lewis, ... 1708
Richard Hayes, ... 1708
John Hood, ... 1708
Thomas Pearson, ... 1708
William Bartram, ... 1708
Daniel Hoopes, ... 1708
Samuel Levis, ... 1709
John Maris, ... 1709
John Hood, ... 1709
Henry Lewis, ... 1709
Daniel Williamson, ... 1709
Daniel Hoopes, ... 1709
Richard Hayes, ... 1709
William Smith, ... 1709
Nicholas Pyle, ... 1710
Joseph Baker, ... 1710
William Lewis, ... 1710
John Wood, ... 1710
Nathaniel Newlin, ... 1710
Ephraim Jackson, ... 1710
Caleb Pusey, ... 1710
Isaac Taylor, ... 1710
Francis Yarnall, ... 1711
John Bezar, ... 1711
Caleb Pusey, ... 1711
Nicholas Pyle, ... 1711
Nathaniel Newlin, ... 1711
Joseph Baker, ... 1711
Nicholas Fairlamb, ... 1711

David Llewelin,	1711
Caleb Pusey,	1712
David Lloyd,	1712
William Davis,	1712
Nicholas Fairlamb,	1712
John Wood,	1712
George Harlan,	1712
Isaac Taylor,	1712
John Maris,	1712
David Lloyd,	1713
William Davis,	1713
Joseph Baker,	1713
Nathaniel Newlin,	1713
Nicholas Fairlamb,	1713
Richard Hayes,	1713
William Brinton,	1713
John Blunston, Jr.,	1713
David Lloyd, Speaker,	1714
Nathaniel Newlin,	1714
Nicholas Pyle,	1714
Evan Lewis,	1714
John Miller, deceased,	1714
Benjamin Mendenhall,	1714
Samuel Garrett,	1714
Richard Maris,	1714
Gawin Miller, vice John Miller, deceased,	1714
David Lloyd,	1715
Samuel Garrett,	1715
Henry Lewis,	1715
Henry Hayes,	1715
William Pyle,	1715
Edward Bezar,	1715
Philip Taylor,	1715
David Lewis,	1715
David Lloyd,	1716
John Blunston, Jr., (deceased,)	1716
Henry Hayes,	1716
Joseph Pennock,	1716
David Harry,	1716
John Maris,	1716
John Worrall,	1716
Henry Oborn,	1716
David Lloyd,	1717
Nathaniel Newlin,	1717
Richard Hayes,	1717
Samuel Garrett,	1717

James Gibbons, ... 1717
John Wood, ... 1717
George Maris, ... 1717
Henry Miller, ... 1717
David Lloyd, ... 1718
Richard Hayes, ... 1718
Nathaniel Newlin, ... 1718
John Wright, ... 1718
James Gibbons, ... 1718
Henry Lewis, ... 1718
William Lewis, ... 1718
Henry Oborn, ... 1718
Isaac Taylor, ... 1719
Joseph Pennock, ... 1719
Joseph Key, ... 1719
John Bezar, ... 1719
Nathaniel Newlin, ... 1719
John Maris, ... 1719
James Gibbons, ... 1719
Evan Lewis, ... 1719
Joseph Pennock, ... 1720
Samuel Levis, Jr., ... 1720
Isaac Taylor, ... 1720
Israel Taylor, ... 1720
John Maris, ... 1720
Ralph Pyle, ... 1720
Daniel Williamson, ... 1720
David Lewis, ... 1720
Samuel Levis, Jr., ... 1721
William Pyle, ... 1721
Daniel Williamson, ... 1721
Isaac Taylor, ... 1721
David Lewis, ... 1721
Henry Oborn, ... 1721
Nathaniel Newlin, ... 1721
Israel Taylor, ... 1721
Samuel Levis, Jr., ... 1722
Joseph Pennock, ... 1722
David Lewis, ... 1722
William Pyle, ... 1722
Daniel Williamson, ... 1722
Israel Taylor, ... 1722
Nathaniel Newlin, ... 1722
Isaac Taylor, ... 1722
Thomas Chandler, ... 1723
Samuel Levis, Jr., ... 1723

Samuel Nutt, ... 1723
John Crosby, ... 1723
Moses Key, ... 1723
William Webb, ... 1723
Joseph Pennock, ... 1723
David Lloyd, ... 1723
Moses Key, ... 1724
Joseph Pennock, ... 1724
William Webb, ... 1724
William Pyle, ... 1724
Thomas Chandler, ... 1724
Elisha Gatchell, ... 1724
John Parry, ... 1724
John Crosby, ... 1724
Thomas Chandler, ... 1725
David Lloyd, Speaker, ... 1725
William Webb, ... 1725
John Wright, ... 1725
Samuel Hollingsworth, ... 1725
William Pusey, ... 1725
George Ashton, ... 1725
William Paschall, ... 1725
David Lloyd, Speaker, ... 1726
Samuel Nutt, ... 1726
Samuel Hollingsworth, ... 1726
John Wright, ... 1726
Richard Hayes, ... 1726
Joseph Pennock, ... 1726
Thomas Chandler, ... 1726
William Pusey, ... 1726
John Parry, ... 1727
Samuel Hollingsworth, ... 1727
David Lloyd, Speaker, ... 1727
Thomas Chandler, ... 1727
John Carter, ... 1727
Daniel Williamson, ... 1727
Simon Meredith, ... 1727
William Webb, ... 1727
Thomas Chandler, ... 1728
David Lloyd, Speaker, ... 1728
Samuel Hollingsworth, ... 1728
John Parry, ... 1728
William Webb, ... 1728
Philip Taylor, ... 1728
John Carter, ... 1728
Henry Hayes, ... 1728

Caleb Cowpland, ...	1729
Richard Hayes, ...	1729
Joseph Brinton, ...	1729
Thomas Chandler, ...	1729
William Webb, ...	1729
Samuel Gilpin, ...	1729
James James, ...	1729
Joseph Pennock, ...	1729
Henry Pierce, ...	1730
John Taylor, ...	1730
Samuel Lewis, ...	1730
John Parry, ...	1730
Thomas Chandler, ...	1730
Samuel Gilpin, ...	1730
William Webb, ...	1730
Henry Hayes, ...	1730
Joseph Harvey, ...	1731
John Parry, ...	1731
Samuel Lewis, ...	1731
Caleb Cowpland, ...	1731
John Taylor, ...	1731
Joseph Brinton, ...	1731
Henry Pierce, ...	1731
Evan Lewis, ...	1731
Caleb Cowpland, ...	1732
Joseph Harvey, ...	1732
Joseph Brinton, ...	1732
Thomas Thomas, ...	1732
William Webb, ...	1732
Joseph Pennock, ...	1732
John Davis, ...	1732
William Hughes, ...	1732
Caleb Cowpland, ...	1733
Joseph Harvey, ...	1733
Joseph Brinton, ...	1733
John Davis, ...	1733
Thomas Thomas, ...	1733
Joseph Pennock, ...	1733
John Owen, ...	1733
William Moore, ...	1733
Joseph Harvey, ...	1734
Joseph Brinton, ...	1734
Caleb Cowpland, ...	1734
John Evans, ...	1734
William Webb, ...	1734
William Moore, ...	1734

John Owen, ... 1734
Joseph Pennock, ... 1734
Joseph Harvey, ... 1735
William Moore, ... 1735
Joseph Pennock, ... 1735
Caleb Cowpland, ... 1735
John Evans, ... 1735
John Parry, ... 1735
Joseph Brinton, ... 1735
Thomas Cummings, ... 1735
Joseph Harvey, ... 1736
Thomas Cummings, ... 1736
John Evans, ... 1736
Caleb Cowpland, ... 1736
William Webb, ... 1736
William Moore, ... 1736
Thomas Chandler, ... 1736
John Parry, ... 1736
Thomas Chandler, ... 1737
Joseph Harvey, ... 1737
John Evans, ... 1737
Thomas Cummings, ... 1737
William Moore, ... 1737
James Gibbons, ... 1737
William Hughes, ... 1737
Richard Hayes, ... 1737
William Moore, ... 1738
James Gibbons, ... 1738
Thomas Chandler, ... 1738
Joseph Harvey, ... 1738
John Owen, ... 1738
Thomas Tatnall, ... 1738
William Hughes, ... 1738
Jeremiah Starr, ... 1738
James Gibbons, ... 1739
Thomas Chandler, ... 1739
Joseph Harvey, ... 1739
William Hughes, ... 1739
Jeremiah Starr, ... 1739
William Moore, ... 1739
Samuel Levis, ... 1739
John Owen, ... 1739
Thomas Chandler, ... 1740
Joseph Harvey, ... 1740
James Gibbons, ... 1740
William Hughes, ... 1740

Samuel Levis,	1740
John Owen,	1740
Jeremiah Starr,	1740
Thomas Tatnall,	1740
Joseph Harvey,	1741
Thomas Chandler,	1741
James Gibbons,	1741
John Owen,	1741
Thomas Tatnall,	1741
Samuel Levis,	1741
William Hughes,	1741
Jeremiah Starr,	1741
James Gibbons,	1742
John Owen,	1742
Samuel Levis,	1742
Jeremiah Starr,	1742
Thomas Chandler,	1742
Joseph Harvey,	1742
William Hughes,	1742
Thomas Tatnall,	1742
Jeremiah Starr,	1743
James Gibbons,	1743
Thomas Chandler,	1743
Joseph Harvey,	1743
Samuel Levis,	1743
Joseph Pennock,	1743
George Ashbridge, Jr.,	1743
Francis Yarnall,	1743
George Ashbridge,	1744
Francis Yarnall,	1744
Joseph Pennock,	1744
Samuel Levis,	1744
James Gibbons,	1744
Joseph Harvey,	1744
Thomas Cummings,	1744
Thomas Chandler,	1744
Joseph Pennock,	1745
Thomas Cummings,	1745
George Ashbridge,	1745
Francis Yarnell,	1745
Robert Lewis,	1745
Joseph Harvey,	1745
Samuel Levis,	1745
Thomas Chandler,	1745
Francis Yarnall,	1746
George Ashbridge,	1746

93

Robert Lewis,	1746
Thomas Worth,	1746
Samuel Levis,	1746
Peter Dix,	1746
Thomas Chandler,	1746
John Owen,	1746
Samuel Levis,	1747
Francis Yarnall,	1747
George Ashbridge,	1747
Thomas Worth,	1747
Peter Dix,	1747
John Owen,	1747
John Davis,	1747
Thomas Chandler,	1747
Thomas Worth,	1748
George Ashbridge,	1748
Francis Yarnall,	1748
John Davis,	1748
Jown Owen,	1748
Joseph James,	1748
Thomas Chandler,	1748
Joseph Gibbons,	1748
Joseph Gibbons,	1749
George Ashbridge,	1749
Henry Hockley,	1749
Thomas Chandler,	1749
Nathaniel Grubb,	1749
Nathaniel Pennock,	1749
Roger Hunt,	1749
Thomas Cummings,	1749
Joseph Gibbons,	1750
George Ashbridge,	1750
Thomas Cummings,	1750
Henry Hockley,	1750
Thomas Chandler,	1750
Nathaniel Grubb,	1750
Nathaniel Pennock,	1750
Peter Dix,	1750
Joseph Gibbons,	1751
Thomas Cummings,	1751
George Ashbridge,	1751
Nathaniel Grubb,	1751
Peter Dix,	1751
Nathaniel Pennock,	1751
Henry Hockley,	1751
Thomas Chandler,	1751

Joseph Gibbons, ...	1752
Thomas Cummings, ...	1752
Nathaniel Pennock, ...	1752
Peter Dix, ...	1752
George Ashbridge, ...	1752
Nathaniel Grubb, ...	1752
William Peters, ...	1752
Jacob Howell, ...	1752
Thomas Cummings, ...	1753
Nathaniel Pennock, ...	1753
George Ashbridge, ...	1753
Joseph Gibbons, ...	1753
Nathaniel Grubb, ...	1753
Peter Dix, ...	1753
William Peters, ...	1753
Joseph James, ...	1753
George Ashbridge, ...	1754
Joseph Gibbons, ...	1754
Peter Dix, ...	1754
Thomas Cummings, ...	1754
Nathaniel Pennock, ...	1754
Nathaniel Grubb, ...	1754
Joseph James, ...	1754
William Peters, ...	1754
Thomas Cummings, ...	1755
George Ashbridge, ...	1755
Nathaniel Pennock, ...	1755
Joseph James, ...	1755
Joseph Gibbons, ...	1755
Nathaniel Grubb, ...	1755
William Peters, ...	1755
Peter Dix, ...	1755
Joseph Gibbons, ...	1756
Peter Dix, ...	1756
John Morton, ...	1756
Roger Hunt, ...	1756
George Ashbridge, ...	1756
Hugh Trimble, ...	1756
Nathaniel Pennock, ...	1756
Nathaniel Grubb, ...	1756
Joseph Gibbons, ...	1757
George Ashbridge, ...	1757
John Morton, ...	1757
Roger Hunt, ...	1757
Isaac Wayne, ...	1757
Nathaniel Grubb, ...	1757

Hugh Trimble,	1757
Joshua Ash,	1757
Joseph Gibbons,	1758
John Morton,	1758
George Ashbridge,	1758
Roger Hunt,	1758
Hugh Trimble,	1758
Joshua Ash,	1758
Nathaniel Grubb,	1758
Isaac Wayne,	1758
John Morton,	1759
George Ashbridge,	1759
Joshua Ash,	1759
Joseph Gibbons,	1759
Hugh Trimble,	1759
Roger Hunt,	1759
Peter Dicks,	1759
Isaac Wayne,	1759
George Ashbridge,	1760
John Morton,	1760
Roger Hunt,	1760
Joshua Ash,	1760
Joseph Gibbons,	1760
Nathaniel Pennock,	1760
Isaac Wayne,	1760
William Boyd,	1760
Joseph Gibbons,	1761
George Ashbridge,	1761
Nathaniel Pennock,	1761
Joshua Ash,	1761
John Morton,	1761
Isaac Wayne,	1761
Isaac Pearson,	1761
Roger Hunt,	1761
Nathaniel Pennock,	1762
George Ashbridge,	1762
Joshua Ash,	1762
Isaac Pearson,	1762
John Morton,	1762
Isaac Wayne,	1762
Joseph Gibbons,	1762
John Jacobs,	1762
George Ashbridge,	1763
Joshua Ash,	1763
Isaac Pearson,	1763
John Morton,	1763

Nathaniel Pennock, ... 1763
John Jacobs, ... 1763
Isaac Wayne, ... 1763
Charles Humphreys, ... 1763
George Ashbridge, ... 1764
John Morton, ... 1764
Nathaniel Pennock, ... 1764
Joshua Ash, ... 1764
Isaac Pearson, ... 1764
Charles Humphreys, ... 1764
John Jacobs, ... 1764
John Fairlamb, ... 1764
John Morton, ... 1765
George Ashbridge, ... 1765
John Jacobs, ... 1765
Nathaniel Pennock, ... 1765
John Fairlamb, ... 1765
Charles Humphreys, ... 1765
Isaac Pearson, ... 1765
Joshua Ash, ... 1765
John Morton, ... 1766
George Ashbridge, ... 1766
Nathaniel Pennock, ... 1766
John Jacobs, ... 1766
Charles Humphreys, ... 1766
Isaac Pearson, ... 1766
Joshua Ash, ... 1766
John Minshall, ... 1766
Isaac Pearson, ... 1767
Charles Humphreys, ... 1767
George Ashbridge, ... 1767
John Minshall, ... 1767
Jonas Preston, ... 1767
John Jacobs, ... 1767
John Sellers, ... 1767
Nathaniel Pennock, ... 1767
John Jacobs, ... 1768
Nathaniel Pennock, ... 1768
George Ashbridge, ... 1768
Charles Humphreys, ... 1768
John Sellers, ... 1768
John Minshall, ... 1768
Isaac Pearson, ... 1768
John Crosby, ... 1768
George Ashbridge, ... 1769
Charles Humphreys, ... 1769

97

Isaac Pearson,	1769
John Sellers,	1769
John Jacobs,	1769
John Minshall,	1769
John Crosby,	1769
John Morton,	1769
Charles Humphreys,	1770
Isaac Pearson,	1770
John Minshall,	1770
John Morton,	1770
John Jacobs,	1770
John Crosby,	1770
George Ashbridge,	1770
John Sellers,	1770
John Morton,	1771
Charles Humphreys,	1771
Isaac Pearson,	1771
John Jacobs,	1771
John Sellers,	1771
John Minshall,	1771
George Ashbridge,	1771
John Crosby,	1771
Charles Humphreys,	1772
Isaac Pearson,	1772
John Morton,	1772
John Jacobs,	1772
John Minshall,	1772
James Hockley,	1772
George Ashbridge,	1772
Benjamin Bartholomew,	1772
Isaac Pearson,	1773
Benjamin Bartholomew,	1773
John Jacobs,	1773
Charles Humphreys,	1773
John Morton,	1773
James Gibbs,	1773
John Minshall,	1773
Joseph Pennock,	1773
Benjamin Bartholomew,	1774
John Jacobs,	1774
Joseph Pennock,	1774
James Gibbons,	1774
Isaac Pearson,	1774
Charles Humphreys,	1774
John Morton,	1774
Anthony Wayne,	1774

John Morton, Speaker,	1775
Benjamin Bartholomew,	1775
James Gibbons,	1775
Isaac Pearson,	1775
John Jacobs,	1775
Charles Humphreys,	1775
Joseph Pennock,	1775
Joseph Pyle,	1775

OFFICERS OF PHILADELPHIA COUNTY.

Sheriffs.

John Test, (merchant of London,)	1682
Benjamin Chambers,	1683
Samuel Hersent, (see Col. Rec., vol. i,)	
William Carter,	Sept. 19, 1686
John Claypoole,	Sept. 18, 1687–89
John White,	1690
John Claypoole,	April 29, 1693–98
Thomas Farmer,	1701, resigned June 10, 1703
John Finney,	June 10, 1703–Dec. 11, 1704
Benjamin Wright,	Oct. 8, 1705
Peter Evans,	April 18, 1707–1714
Owen Roberts,	1716–1721
Owen Owen,	Oct. 4, 1726; Oct. 4, 1727; Oct. 3, 1728
Charles Read,	Oct. 4, 1729; Oct. 3, 1730; Oct. 4, 1731
Septimus Robinson,	1732–3–4
Joseph Brientnall,	1735–6–7
Septimus Robinson,	1738–9–40
John Hyatt,	1741–2–3
Nicholas Scull,	1744–5–6
Richard Sewell,	1747–8–9
Isaac Griffitts,	1750–51
Samuel Morris,	March 9, 1752; Oct. 4, 1752–3–4
James Coultas,	1755–6–8
Samuel Morris,	1759–60
Joseph Redman,	1761–2–3
William Parr,	1764–5–6
Joseph Redman,	1767–8–9
Judah Foulke,	1770–1–2
William Dewees,	1773–4–5

Deputy Sheriffs and Keepers of the Gaol.

William Tonge,	1701–2
John Andrews,	1704

99

David Evans, ... 1714–21
William Biddle, ... 1738
Thomas Croasdale, ... 1742-3-4
James Whitehead, (keeper of work-house,) . . . 1749
John Mitchell, ... 1763

Coroners.

Griffith Owen, ... 1685
Henry Lewis, (resigned,) . . . . . . March, 1686
Thomas Fitzwater, ... July, 25, 1688
Wiliam Lee, ... Oct. 16, 1703
Richard Walker, ... 1713–1715
Enoch Story, ... 1715–1717
Richard Walker, ... 1717–1720
Merrick Davis, ... Oct. 4, 1720
Joshua Fincher, (died Aug. 1728,) 1726–1728
James Macky, (*vice* Fincher, deceased,) . . . Sept. 1, 1728
Merrick Davis, ... Oct. 3, 1728
Owen Owen, ... 1729–1741
Henry Pratt, ... 1741–1749
George Heap, ... 1749–1751
Thomas James, ... 1751–1754
Thomas Boude, ... 1754–1759
Peter Robeson, ... 1759–1763
Caleb Cash, (died Feb., 1773,) 1763–1773
John Knight, (*vice* Caleb Cash, deceased,) . . 1773–1775
Robert Jewell, ... Oct. 5, 1775

Recorders.

Thomas Story, appointed in the charter, ... 1701
David Lloyd, (*vice* Story, resigned,) 1702
Robert Assheton, (*vice* Lloyd, resigned,) . . Aug. 3, 1708
Charles Brockden, ... 1722
Andrew Hamilton, (*vice* Assheton, deceased,) . June 12, 1727
Thomas Hopkinson, (*vice* Hamilton, deceased,) . June 20, 1736
William Allen, ... Aug. 7, 1741
Tench Francis, (*vice* Allen, resigned,) . . . Oct. 2, 1750
Benjamin Chew, (*vice* Francis, resigned,) . . Aug. 29, 1755
William Parr, (*vice* Chew, resigned,) . . . Oct. 3, 1767
Andrew Allen, ... June 25, 1774

Register.

Peter Evans, (Deputy Register,) . . . . April 3, 1706
Charles Read, (Clerk of Orphans' Court,) . . 1721
Thomas Hopkinson, (*vice* Read, deceased,) . . Jan. 20, 1736-7
John Price, (Clerk of Orphans Court, *vice* Hopkin-
son, deceased,) . . . . Feb. 28, 1752
James Humphreys, (Clerk of Orphans' Court, *vice*
Price, resigned.) (See Col. Rec., vol. vii, p. 501,) May 7, 1757

Post-Master.

Colonel And. Hamilton, ... 1699

Surveyor.

David Powel, ... Dec. 2, 1706

Deputy Surveyors.

Robert Turner, ... Sept. 19, 1686
John Barnes, ... Sept. 19, 1686

Overseer of Highways.

Humphrey Parker, in township of Lower Dublin, March 2, 1710–11

Sealer of Weights and Measures.

Judah Foulke, ... Dec. 9, 1773

Collectors of Money granted Proprietary.

Thomas Farmer, ... March 28, 1704
John Furness, ... March 28, 1704
William Tonge.
John Joyce, collector of arrears of said tax, . May 23, 1704

Town Clerks.

David Lloyd.
Robert Assheton, ... 1701 to 1709
Ralph Assheton, ... 1733–34

Clerks of the Courts.

Robert Assheton, ... 1709–1726
Ralph Assheton, ... 1733–34

Prothonotaries.

Robert Assheton, ... 1722–23
Andrew Hamilton, ... June 5, 1727
James Hamilton, ... Dec. 28, 1733
Thomas Hopkinson, ... Nov. 24, 1748
James Read, ... May 1, 1752
James Hamilton, ... 1754–1764

Clerks of the Peace.

John Lawrence, ... Sept. 8, 1747
James Read, ... June 4, 1752

Ranger.

John Barnes, ... Nov. 9, 1685

Attorney.

Samuel Hersent, (commission revoked,) . . Dec.	1, 1685

Clerks to County Commissioners.

John Southern.
Patrick Robinson, (dismissed.)
David Lloyd, (dismissed,) . . . . . Aug. 1, 1686
James Claypoole, ... Jan. 1, 1689

Treasurers.

Benjamin Chambers, Deputy Treasurer, . . Feb. 22, 1684
Evan Owen, ... 1724-5-6
William Fishbourne, City Treasurer, . . 1725-6
Thomas Leech, ... 1757-8-9
Philip Syng, ... 1759 to 1769
Barnaby Barnes, ... 1769 to 1776

Justices of the Peace.

William Clayton, ... Aug. 19, 1684
Robert Turner, ... Aug. 19, 1684
Francis Daniel Pastorius, ... Aug. 19, 1684
James Claypoole, ... Nov. 6, 1685
William Frampton, ... Nov. 6, 1685
Humphrey Murray, ... Nov. 6, 1685
William Salway, ... Nov. 6, 1685
John Bevan, ... Nov. 6, 1685
Lace Cock, ... Nov. 6, 1685
William Wardner, Sr., ... Nov. 6, 1685
Robert Turner, ... Nov. 6, 1685
John Moran, ... Nov. 6, 1685
Christopher Taylor, Jr., ... May 17, 1686
William Southerby, ... Sept. 20, 1686
Barnaby Wilcox, ... Sept. 20, 1686
John Eckley, ... May 18, 1687
John Goodson, ... May 18, 1687
Barnabas Wilcox, ... May 18, 1687
John Shelton, ... May 18, 1687
Thomas Ellis, ... May 18, 1687
William Southerby, ... May 18, 1687
Joshua Cart, ... May 18, 1687
Thomas Lloyd, ... Jan. 2, 1689
John Eckley, ... Jan. 2, 1689
Robert Turner, ... Jan. 2, 1689
William Salway, ... Jan. 2, 1689
Barnaby Wilcox, ... Jan. 2, 1689
Francis Rawle, ... Jan. 2, 1689

Lawrence Cock,	Jan.	2, 1689
John Holme,	Jan.	2, 1689
Arthur Cook,	Sept.	6, 1690
Arthur Cook,	Sept.	6, 1692
Samuel Richardson,	Sept.	6, 1692
Anthony Morris,	Sept.	6, 1692
Robert Einer,	Sept.	6, 1692
William Salway,	May	5, 1693
Anthony Morris,	May	6, 1693
Jacob Hall,	May	6, 1693
Griffith Owen, (declined,)	May	6, 1693
Andrew Bankson,	May	6, 1693
Francis Rawle,	May	6, 1693
Francis Daniel Pastorius,	May	6, 1693
Humphrey Waterman,	May	10, 1693
Joshua Carpenter,	May	18, 1693
Edward Shippen,		1697
Charles Sober,		1697
James Fox,		1697
Anthony Morris,		1697
John Farmer,		1697
Samuel Richardson,		1697
Nathan Stanbury,		1700
John Jones,		1700
John Guest,	Sept.	2, 1701
Robert French,	Sept.	2, 1701
Nathan Stanbury,	Sept.	2, 1701
Samuel Finney,	Sept.	2, 1701
Samuel Richardson,	Sept.	2, 1701
John Jones,	Sept.	2, 1701
Edward Farmer,	Jan.	29, 1703
Andrew Bankson,	Jan.	29, 1703
Rowland Ellis,	Jan.	29, 1703
John Guest,	Sept.	4, 1704
Samuel Finney,	Sept.	4, 1704
George Roach,	Sept.	4, 1704
Samuel Richardson,	Sept.	4, 1704
Nathan Stanbury,	Sept.	4, 1704
John Jones,	Sept.	4, 1704
Joseph Pidgeon,	Sept.	4, 1704
Edward Farmer,	Sept.	4, 1704
Rowland Ellis,	Sept.	4, 1704
Andrew Bankson, Jr.,	Sept.	4, 1704
Joseph Pidgeon,	June	5, 1708
Richard Hill,	June	4, 1715
Isaac Norris,	June	4, 1715

James Logan,	June	4, 1715
Nathan Stanbury,	June	4, 1715
Edward Farmer,	June	4, 1715
Rowland Ellis,	June	4, 1715
Benjamin Vining,	June	4, 1715
Josiah Rolfe,	June	4, 1715
Richard Hill,	Sept.	1, 1715
James Logan,	Sept.	1, 1715
Edward Farmer,	Sept.	1, 1715
Benjamin Vining,	Sept.	1, 1715
Richard Anthony,	Sept.	1, 1715
Robert Jones,	Sept.	1, 1715
Isaac Morris,	Sept.	1, 1715
Nathan Stanbury,	Sept.	1, 1715
Rowland Ellis,	Sept.	1, 1715
Josiah Rolfe,	Sept.	1, 1715
John Swift,	Sept.	1, 1715
Richard Hill,	Aug.	19, 1718
Isaac Morris,	Aug.	19, 1718
Robert Ashton,	Aug.	19, 1718
Nathan Stanbury,	Aug.	19, 1718
Rowland Ellis,	Aug.	19, 1718
Josiah Rolfe,	Aug.	19, 1718
John Swift,	Aug.	19, 1718
Andrew Hamilton,	Aug.	19, 1718
James Logan,	Aug.	19, 1718
Jonathan Dickinson,	Aug.	19, 1718
Anthony Palmer,	Aug.	19, 1718
Edward Farmer,	Aug.	19, 1718
Benjamin Vining,	Aug.	19, 1718
Clement Plumstead,	Aug.	19, 1718
Robert Jones, (Merion,)	Aug.	19, 1718
William Fishbourne,	Dec.	5, 1719
Richard Hill,	Dec.	5, 1719
Isaac Norris,	Dec.	5, 1719
Robert Ashton,	Dec.	5, 1719
Nathan Stanbury,	Dec.	5, 1719
Rowland Ellis,	Dec.	5, 1719
Josiah Rolfe,	Dec.	5, 1719
John Swift,	Dec.	5, 1719
Andrew Hamilton,	Dec.	5, 1719
James Logan,	Dec.	5, 1719
Jonathan Dickinson,	Dec.	5, .719
Anthony Palmer,	Dec.	5, 1719
Edward Farmer,	Dec.	5, 1719
Benjamin Vining,	Dec.	5, 1719

Clement Plumstead,	Dec.	5, 1719
Robert Jones, (Merion,)	Dec.	5, 1719
Richard Hill,	June	14, 1722
Jonathan Dickinson,	June	14, 1722
Robert Ashton,	June	14, 1722
Edward Farmer,	June	14, 1722
Benjamin Vining,	June	14, 1722
John Swift,	June	14, 1722
Samuel Carpenter,	June	14, 1722
Rees Thomas,	June	14, 1722
James Logan,	June	14, 1722
Isaac Norris,	June	14, 1722
William Fishbourne,	June	14, 1722
Anthony Palmer,	June	14, 1722
Rowland Ellis,	June	14, 1722
Clement Plumstead,	June	14, 1722
Robert Jones, (North Wales,)	June	14, 1722
Charles Read,	June	14, 1722
Francis Rawle,	June	14, 1722
Robert Fletcher,	June	14, 1722
John Swift,	June	4, 1715
Samuel Carpenter,	June	4, 1715
Joseph Fisher,	June	4, 1715
Robert Jones,	June	4, 1715
The Major and Recorder of the City,	June	4, 1715
Richard Hill,	Sept.	2, 1717
James Logan,	Sept.	2, 1717
Nathan Stanbury,	Sept.	2, 1717
Rowland Ellis,	Sept.	2, 1717
Josiah Rolfe,	Sept.	2, 1717
Robert Jones,	Sept.	2, 1717
Morris Morris,	Sept.	2, 1717
Isaac Norris,	Sept.	2, 1717
Anthony Palmer,	Sept.	2, 1717
Edward Farmer,	Sept.	2, 1717
Benjamin Vining,	Sept.	2, 1717
John Swift,	Sept.	2, 1717
Clement Plumsted,	Sept.	2, 1717
The Mayor and Recorder,	Sept.	2, 1717
Samuel Peres,	Aug.	19, 1718
Richard Moore,	Aug.	19, 1718
Robert Jones, (North Wales,)	Aug.	19, 1718
Samuel Carpenter,	Aug.	19, 1718
Charles Read,	Aug.	19, 1718
Josiah Rolfe,	Feb.	18, 1723
Robert Fletcher,	Feb.	18, 1723

Richard Alborough,	Feb.	18, 1723
Thomas Lawrence,	Feb.	18, 1723
Evan Owen,	Feb.	18, 1723
John Cadwalader,	Feb.	18, 1723
Edward Roberts,	Feb.	18, 1723
Richard Hill,	May	12, 1725
Isaac Norris,	May	12, 1725
Robert Asheton,	May	12, 1725
Anthony Palmer,	May	12, 1725
William Fishbourne,	May	12, 1725
Edward Farmer,	May	12, 1725
Clement Plumsted,	May	12, 1725
John Swift,	May	12, 1725
Robert Jones, (North Wales,)	May	12, 1725
Samuel Carpenter,	May	12, 1725
Charles Read,	May	12, 1725
Rees Thomas,	May	12, 1725
Francis Rawle,	May	12, 1725
Robert Fisher,	May	12, 1725
Robert Fletcher,	May	12, 1725
Thomas Lawrence,	May	12, 1725
Evan Owen,	May	12, 1725
John Cadwalader,	May	12, 1725
Edward Roberts,	May	12, 1725
Isaac Norris,	Aug.	25, 1726
James Logan,	Aug.	25, 1726
Anthony Palmer,	Aug.	25, 1726
Samuel Preston,	Aug.	25, 1726
William Fishbourne,	Aug.	25, 1726
Edward Farmer,	Aug.	25, 1726
Clement Plumsted,	Aug.	25, 1726
John Swift,	Aug.	25, 1726
Charles Read,	Aug.	25, 1726
Robert Fletcher,	Aug.	25, 1726
Thomas Lawrence,	Aug.	25, 1726
Evan Owen,	Aug.	25, 1726
Edward Roberts,	Aug.	25, 1726
Thomas Fenton,	Aug.	25, 1726
Richard Harrison,	Aug.	25, 1726
Josheph Ashton,	Aug.	25, 1726
Derrick Jansen,	Aug.	25, 1726
Owen Evans, (of North Wales,)	Aug.	25, 1726
Isaac Norris,	Sept.	2, 1727
James Logan,	Sept.	2, 1727
Anthony Palmer,	Sept.	2, 1727
William Fishbourne,	Sept.	2, 1727

Clement Plumsted, ...	Sept.	2, 1727
Edward Farmer, ...	Sept.	2, 1727
John Swift, ...	Sept.	2, 1727
Charles Read, ...	Sept.	2, 1727
Thomas Lawrence, ...	Sept.	2, 1727
Edward Roberts, ...	Sept.	2, 1727
Thomas Fenton, ...	Sept.	2, 1727
Richard Harrison, ...	Sept.	2, 1727
Joseph Asheton, ...	Sept.	2, 1727
Derrick Jansen, ...	Sept.	2, 1727
Owen Evans, ...	Sept.	2, 1727
George Boone, ...	Mar.	5, 1728
William Allen, ...	April	20, 1730
Thomas Lawrence, ...	Oct.	26, 1730
Clement Plumsted, ...	Oct.	26, 1730
Thomas Griffitts, ...	Oct.	14, 1731
Isaac Norris, ...	Mar.	5, 1732-3
Clement Plumsted, ...	Mar.	5, 1732-3
Thomas Lawrence, ...	Mar.	5, 1732-3
Samuel Hasell, ...	Mar.	5, 1732-3
The Mayor of the City, for the time being, .	Mar.	5, 1732-3
The Recorder of the City, for the time being, .	Mar.	5, 1732-3
Edward Farmer, ...	Mar.	5, 1732-3
Charles Read, ...	Mar.	5, 1732-3
Edward Roberts, ...	Mar.	5, 1732-3
Richard Harrison, ...	Mar.	5, 1732-3
Derrick Jansen, ...	Mar.	5, 1732-3
Owen Evans, ...	Mar.	5, 1732-3
William Allen, ...	Mar.	5, 1732-3
George Boone, ...	Mar.	5, 1732-3
Thomas Griffitts, ...	Mar.	5, 1732-3
George Fitzwater, ...	Mar.	5, 1732-3
Richard Martin, ...	Mar.	5, 1732-3
Lasse Bore, ...	Mar.	5, 1732-3
John Pawling, ...	Mar.	5, 1732-3
Mordecai Lincoln, ...	Mar.	5, 1732-3
Isaac Norris, ...	Dec.	3, 1733
Clement Plumsted, ...	Dec.	3, 1733
Thomas Lawrence, ...	Dec.	3, 1733
Samuel Hasell, ...	Dec.	3, 1733
Thomas Griffitts, ...	Dec.	3, 1733
Charles Read, ...	Dec.	3, 1733
Edward Farmer, ...	Dec.	3, 1733
Edward Roberts, ...	Dec.	3, 1733
Richard Harrison, ...	Dec.	3, 1733
Derrick Jansen, ...	Dec.	3, 1733

Owen Evans, ...	Dec. 3, 1733
William Allen, ...	Dec. 3, 1733
George Boone, ...	Dec. 3, 1733
George Fitzwater, ...	Dec. 3, 1733
Richard Martin, ...	Dec. 3, 1733
John Pawlin, ...	Dec. 3, 1733
Mordecai Lincoln, ...	Dec. 3, 1733
Evan Thomas, ...	Dec. 3, 1733
Henry Pastorius, ...	Dec. 3, 1733
Ralph Assheton, ...	Feb. 23, 173$\frac{4}{5}$
Clement Plumsted, ...	Feb. 23, 173$\frac{4}{5}$
Samuel Hasell, ...	Feb. 23, 173$\frac{4}{5}$
Thomas Griffitts, ...	Feb. 23, 173$\frac{4}{5}$
Thomas Lawrence, ...	Feb. 23, 173$\frac{4}{5}$
Ralph Assheton, ...	Feb. 23, 173$\frac{4}{5}$
The Mayor of Philadelphia, for the time being, .	Feb. 23, 173$\frac{4}{5}$
The Recorder of Philadelphia for the time being, .	Feb. 23, 173$\frac{4}{5}$
Edward Farmer, ...	Feb. 23, 173$\frac{4}{5}$
Richard Harrison, ...	Feb. 23, 173$\frac{4}{5}$
William Allen, ...	Feb. 23, 173$\frac{4}{5}$
George Fitzwater, ...	Feb. 23, 173$\frac{4}{5}$
Edward Roberts, ...	Feb. 23, 173$\frac{4}{5}$
Derrick Jansen, ...	Feb. 23, 173$\frac{4}{5}$
George Boone, ...	Feb. 23, 173$\frac{4}{5}$
Thomas Fletcher.	Dec. 2, 1737
Clement Plumsted, ...	Dec. 2, 1737
Samuel Hasell, ...	Dec. 2, 1737
Thomas Griffitts, ...	Dec. 2, 1737
Thomas Lawrence.	Dec. 2, 1737
Ralph Assheton, ...	Dec. 2, 1737
The Mayor of Philadelphia, for the time being, .	Dec. 2, 1737
The Recorder of Philadelphia, for the time being,	Dec. 2, 1737
Edward Farmer.	Dec. 2, 1737
Richard Harrison, ...	Dec. 2, 1737
William Allen.	Dec. 2, 1737
George Fitzwater, ...	Dec. 2, 1737
Edward Roberts, ...	Dec. 2, 1737
Derrick Jansen, ...	Dec. 2, 1737
George Boone, ...	Dec. 2, 1737
Clement Plumsted, ...	Nov. 22, 1738
Samuel Hasell, ...	Nov. 22, 1738
Thomas Griffitts, ...	Nov. 22, 1738
Thomas Lawrence, ...	Nov. 22, 1738
Ralph Assheton, ...	Nov. 22, 1738
The Mayor of Philadelphia, for the time being, .	Nov. 22, 1738
The Recorder of Philadelphia, for the time being,	Nov. 22, 1738

Edward Farmer,	Nov.	22, 1738
Richard Harrison,	Nov.	22, 1738
William Allen,	Nov.	22, 1738
George Fitzwater,	Nov.	22, 1738
Thomas Fletcher,	Nov.	22, 1738
Cadwalader Foulke,	Nov.	22, 1738
Jonathan Robeson,	Nov.	22, 1738
Edward Roberts,	Nov.	22, 1738
Derrick Jansen,	Nov.	22, 1738
George Boone,	Nov.	22, 1738
James Hamilton,	Nov.	22, 1738
William Till,	Nov.	22, 1738
Abram Taylor,	Nov.	22, 1738
Owen Evans, of Limerick,	Nov.	22, 1738
Edward Reece, of Manhatawney,	Nov.	22. 1738
David Humphreys, of Merion,	Nov.	22, 1738
Clement Plumsted,	April	10, 1741
Thomas Lawrence,	April	10, 1741
Samuel Hasell,	April	10, 1741
Ralph Assheton,	April	10, 1741
The Mayor of Philadelphia for the time being,	April	10, 1741
The Recorder of Philadelphia for the time being,	April	10, 1741
Edward Roberts,	April	10, 1741
Richard Harrison,	April	10, 1741
William Allen,	April	10, 1741
George Boone,	April	10, 1741
George Fitzwater,	April	10, 1741
James Hamilton,	April	10, 1741
William Till,	April	10, 1741
Abram Taylor,	April	10, 1741
Jonathan Robeson,	April	10, 1741
Owen Evans, of Limerick,	April	10, 1741
Isaac Leech,	April	10, 1741
Benjamin Shoemaker,	April	10, 1741
Joseph Paschal,	April	10, 1741
Joshua Maddox,	April	10, 1741
Robert Strettell,	April	10, 1741
Griffith Lewellyn,	April	10, 1741
Derrick Keyser,	April	10, 1741
Abram Taylor,		1742–43
Septimus Robinson,		1742–43
Isaac Norris,		1742–43
Clement Plumsted,		1742–43
Thomas Lawrence,	May	27, 1745
Samuel Hasell,	May	27, 1745
Ralph Assheton,	May	27, 1745

109

Abram Taylor,	May	27, 1745
Robert Strettell,	May	27, 1745
The Mayor of the City for the time being,	May	27, 1745
The Recorder of the City for the time being,	May	27, 1745
William Allen,	May	27, 1745
Richard Harrison,	May	27, 1745
George Boone,	May	27, 1775
George Fitzwater,	May	27, 1745
Jonathan Robeson,	May	27, 1745
Owen Evans,	May	27, 1745
Benjamin Shoemaker,	May	27, 1745
Joshua Maddox,	May	27, 1745
Septimus Robinson,	May	27, 1745
Griffith Lewellyn,	May	27, 1745
Derrick Keyser,	May	27, 1745
Edward Shippen,	May	27, 1745
Joseph Turner,	May	27, 1745
Charles Willing,	May	27, 1745
Thomas Venables,	May	27, 1745
Nicholas Ashton,	May	27, 1745
Thomas Fletcher,	May	27, 1745
Samuel Morris, (of White Marsh,)	May	27, 1745
Thomas York,	May	27, 1745
James Delaplaine,	May	27, 1745
Francis Parvin,	May	27, 1745
John Potts,	May	27, 1745
Anthony Lee,	May	27, 1745
William Peters,	May	3, 1749
Thomas Lawrence,	June	30, 1749
Samuel Hasell,	June	30, 1749
Abram Taylor,	June	30, 1749
Robert Strettell,	June	30, 1749
Benjamin Shoemaker,	June	30, 1749
Joseph Turner,	June	30, 1749
Thomas Hopkinson,	June	30, 1749
William Logan,	June	30, 1749
The Mayor of the City, for the time being,	June	30, 1749
The Recorder of the City, for the time being,	June	30, 1749
William Allen,	June	30, 1749
Jonathan Robeson,	June	30, 1749
Owen Evans,	June	30, 1749
Joshua Maddox,	June	30, 1749
Septimus Robinson,	June	30, 1749
Edward Shippen,	June	30, 1749
Charles Willing,	June	30, 1749
Thomas Venables,	June	30, 1749

Nicholas Ashton,	June	30, 1749
Thomas Fletcher	June	30, 1749
Samuel Morris, (of White Marsh,)	June	30, 1749
Thomas Yorke,	June	30, 1749
Francis Parvin,	June	30, 1749
John Potts,	June	30, 1749
Anthony Lee,	June	30, 1749
William Coleman,	June	30, 1749
Benjamin Franklin,	June	30, 1749
John Smith,	June	30, 1749
Rowland Evans,	June	30, 1749
Samuel Mifflin,	June	—, 1750
Conrad Weiser,	March	25, 1751
Jonas Seely,	March	25, 1751
Thomas Lawrence,	May	25, 1752
Robert Strettell,	May	25, 1752
Benjamin Shoemaker,	May	25, 1752
Joseph Turner,	May	25, 1752
William Logan,	May	25, 1752
The Mayor and Recorder of Philadelphia, for the time being,	May	25, 1752
Owen Evans,	May	25, 1752
Joshua Maddox,	May	25, 1752
Septimus Robinson,	May	25, 1752
Edward Willing,	May	25, 1752
Nicholas Ashton,	May	25, 1752
Thomas Fletcher,	May	25, 1752
John Potts,	May	25, 1752
William Coleman,	May	25, 1752
Benjamin Franklin,	May	25, 1752
John Smith,	May	25, 1752
Rowland Evans,	May	25, 1752
William Plumsted,	May	25, 1752
Thomas White,	May	25, 1752
John Mifflin,	May	25, 1752
Henry Antes,	May	25, 1752
Henry Pawling,	May	25, 1752
Samuel Ashmead,	May	25, 1752
John Jones,	May	25, 1752
Abraham Dawes,	May	25, 1752
Charles Brockden,	Aug.	1, 1752
James Humphreys,	March	28, 1754
Henry Antes,	May	3, 1754
The members of Council,	Nov.	27, 1757
William Coleman,	Nov.	27, 1757
Joshua Maddox,	Nov.	27, 1757

111

Septimus Robinson,	Nov.	27, 1757
John Potts,	Nov.	27, 1757
Rowland Evans,	Nov.	27, 1757
William Plumsted,	Nov.	27, 1757
Henry Pawling,	Nov.	27, 1757
Samuel Ashmead,	Nov.	27, 1757
John Jones,	Nov.	27, 1757
William Peters,	Nov.	27, 1757
Atwood Shute,	Nov.	27, 1757
Alexander Stedman,	Nov.	27, 1757
Samuel Mifflin,	Nov.	27, 1757
Jacob Duché,	Nov.	27, 1757
Isaac Jones,	Nov.	27, 1757
Evan Thomas,	Nov.	27, 1757
John Roberts,	Nov.	27, 1757
Archibald McClean,	Nov.	27, 1757
Enoch Davis,	Nov.	27, 1757
William Dewees,	Nov.	27, 1757
John Koplin,	Nov.	27, 1757
George Evans,	Nov.	27, 1757
Isaac Ashton,	Nov.	27, 1757
James Humphrey,	Oct.	20, 1759
John Hughes,	Oct.	20, 1759
The members of Council,	Feb.	28, 1761
Alexander Stedman,	Feb.	28, 1761
William Plumsted,	Feb.	28, 1761
Septimus Robinson,	Feb.	28, 1761
John Potts, Jr.,	Feb.	28. 1761
Rowland Evans,	Feb.	28, 1761
Henry Pawling,	Feb.	28, 1761
Samuel Ashmead,	Feb.	28, 1761
John Jones, (Germantown,)	Feb.	28, 1761
Willlam Peters,	Feb.	28, 1761
Samuel Mifflin,	Feb.	28, 1761
Jacob Duché,	Feb.	28, 1761
Isaac Jones,	Feb.	28, 1761
William Coxe,	Feb.	28, 1761
Thomas Willing,	Feb.	28, 1761
Daniel Benezet,	Feb.	28, 1761
William Parr,	Feb.	28, 1761
Henry Harrison,	Feb.	28, 1761
Samuel Shoemaker,	Feb.	27, 1761
Edward Penington,	Feb.	28, 1761
Joshua Howell,	Feb.	28, 1761
Evan Thomas,	Feb.	28, 1761
John Roberts, (miller,)	Feb.	28, 1761

Archibald McClean,	Feb.	28, 1761
Enoch Davis,	Feb.	28, 1761
William Dewees,	Feb.	28, 1761
John Koplin,	Feb.	28, 1761
George Evans,	Feb.	28, 1761
Isaac Ashton,	Feb.	28, 1761
Jacob Hall,	Feb.	28, 1761
James Coultas,	Feb.	28, 1761
John Bull,	Feb.	28, 1761
William Maybury,	Feb.	28, 1761
John Trump,	Feb.	28, 1761
James Humphreys,	March	4, 1761
Members of the Council,	Nov.	19, 1764
Jacob Duché,	Nov.	19, 1764
Isaac Jones,	Nov.	19, 1764
William Coxe,	Nov.	19, 1764
Thomas Willing,	Nov.	19, 1764
Daniel Benezet,	Nov.	19, 1764
Samuel Shoemaker,	Nov.	19, 1764
William Parr,	Nov.	19, 1764
Evan Thomas,	Nov.	19, 1764
Archibald McClean,	Nov.	19, 1764
William Dewees,	Nov.	19, 1764
Henry Harrison,	Nov.	19, 1764
James Coultas,	Nov.	19, 1764
Jacob Hall,	Nov.	19, 1764
John Bull,	Nov.	19, 1764
Thomas Lawrence,	Nov.	19, 1764
John Lawrence,	Nov.	19, 1764
George Bryan,	Nov.	19, 1764
William Humphreys,	Nov.	19, 1764
Frederick Antes,	Nov.	19, 1764
Peter Evans,	Nov.	19, 1764
James Biddle,	Nov.	19, 1764
Alexander Edwards,	Nov.	19, 1764
James Humphreys, (special commission,)	Nov.	30, 1764
William Plumsted,	Dec.	3, 1764
Alexander Edwards,	Dec.	3, 1764
Samuel Ashmead,	Dec.	3, 1764
Samuel Mifflin,	Dec.	3, 1764
William Peters,	Dec.	3, 1764
Enoch Davis, (special commission,)	Jan.	17, 1765
William Plumsted,	Jan.	17, 1765
Septimus Robinson,	Jan.	17, 1765
Samuel Ashmead,	Jan.	17, 1765
William Peters,	Jan.	17, 1765

113

Samuel Mifflin,	Jan.	17, 1765
Jacob Duché,	Jan.	17, 1765
Isaac Jones,	Jan.	17, 1765
William Coxe,	Jan.	17, 1765
Thomas Willing,	Jan.	17, 1765
David Benezet,	Jan.	17, 1765
Samuel Shoemaker,	Jan.	17, 1765
William Parr,	Jan.	17, 1765
Evan Thomas,	Jan.	17, 1765
Archibald McClean,	Jan.	17, 1765
William Dewees,	Jan.	17, 1765
Henry Harrison,	Jan.	17, 1765
James Coultas,	Jan.	17, 1765
Jacob Hall,	Jan.	17, 1765
John Bull,	Jan.	17, 1765
Thomas Lawrence,	Jan.	17, 1765
John Lawrence,	Jan.	17, 1765
George Bryan,	Jan.	17, 1765
William Humphreys,	Jan.	17, 1765
Frederick Antes,	Jan.	17, 1765
Peter Evans,	Jan.	17, 1765
James Biddle,	Jan.	17, 1765
Alexander Edwards,	Jan.	17, 1765
John Allen,	March	31, 1767
Charles Jolly,	May	14, 1767
James Young,	May	14, 1767
Charles Jolly,	Sept.	22, 1767
James Young,	Sept.	25, 1767
Charles Batho,	June	25, 1768
Members of Council,	May	23, 1770
Isaac Jones,	May	23, 1770
Samuel Ashmead,	May	23, 1770
Samuel Mifflin,	May	23, 1770
Jacob Duché,	May	23, 1770
Samuel Shoemaker,	May	23, 1770
William Parr,	May	23, 1770
Evan Thomas,	May	23, 1770
Archibald McClean,	May	23, 1770
William Dewees,	May	23, 1770
Jacob Hall,	May	23, 1770
John Bull,	May	23, 1770
Thomas Lawrence,	May	23, 1770
George Bryan,	May	23, 1770
Frederick Antes,	May	23, 1770
James Biddle,	May	23, 1770
Alexander Edwards,	May	23, 1770

John Allen, ...	May	23, 1770
Charles Jolly, ...	May	23, 1770
James Young, ...	May	23, 1770
Charles Batho, ...	May	23, 1770
John Gibson, ...	May	23, 1770
Peter Chevalier, ...	May	23, 1770
Peter Knight, ...	May	23, 1770
John Potts, ...	May	23, 1770
James Humphreys, ...	June	4, 1770
John Moore, ...	Aug.	1, 1771
Matthew Clarkson, ...	Aug.	4, 1771
Peter Miller, ...	Jan.	6, 1772
Members of the council, *ex-officio*, . . .	Jan.	6, 1772
Isaac Jones, ...	April	27, 1772
Samuel Ashmead, ...	April	27, 1772
Samuel Mifflin, ...	April	27, 1772
Jacob Duché, ...	April	27, 1772
Samuel Shoemaker, ...	April	27, 1772
William Parr, ...	April	27, 1772
Archibald McClean, ...	April	27, 1772
John Bull, ...	April	27, 1772
George Bryan, ...	April	27, 1772
Frederick Antes, ...	April	27, 1772
James Biddle, ...	April	27, 1772
Alexander Edwards, ...	April	27, 1772
John Allen, ...	April	27, 1772
James Young, ...	April	27, 1772
John Gibson, ...	April	27, 1772
John Potts, ...	April	27, 1772
John Moore, ...	April	27, 1772
Thomas Rutter, ...	April	27, 1772
James Deimer, ...	April	27, 1772
Samuel Potts, ...	April	27, 1772
George Clymer, ...	April	27, 1772
Samuel Irwin, or Erwin, ...	April	27, 1772
Lindsay Coats, ...	April	27, 1772
Charles Bensel, ...	April	27, 1772
James Humphreys, ...	May	2, 1772
John Ord, ...	May	2, 1772
Henry Hill, ...	May	4, 1772
Samuel Powel, ...	May	4, 1772
Matthew Clarkson, ...	May	6, 1772
Samuel Powel, ...	May	26, 1772
Henry Hill, ...	June	13, 1772
Alexander Wilcocks, ...	Mar.	4, 1774
Henry Hugh Fergusson, ...	Feb.	13, 1775

Assembly.

John Songhurst, (Deputy Speaker, 1683,)	1682–83
John Hart,	1682–83
Walter King,	1682–83
Andrew Bankson,	1682–83
John Moore,	1682–83
Thomas Wynne, (Speaker,)	1682–83
Griffith Jones,	1682–83
William Warner,	1682–83
Swen Swenson,	1682–83
Nicholas Moore, (Speaker,)	1684
John Songhurst,	1684
Francis Fincher,	1684
Lasse Cock,	1684
Joseph Growden,	1684
John Hart,	1694
Nicholas Moore,	1685
Joseph Growden,	1685
Barnaby Wilcox,	1685
Lawrence Cock,	1685
Gunner Rambo,	1685
Thomas Paschall,	1685
James Claypoole,	1686
John Songhurst,	1686
Thomas Duckett,	1686
John Goodson,	1686
Griffith Owen,	1686
Andrew Bankson,	1686
Humphrey Murray,	1687
William Salway,	1687
John Bevan,	1687
Lasse Cock,	1687
Daniel Pastorius,	1687
Joseph Paul,	1687
Thomas Hooton,	1688
Thomas Fitzwater,	1688
Lasse Cock,	1688
James Fox,	1688
Griffith Owen,	1688
William Southerby,	1688
Joseph Fisher,	1689
Abraham Updegrave,	1689
Griffith Owen,	1689
Thomas Paschall,	1689
Thomas Duckett,	1689

Henry Waddy,	1689
William Salway,	1690
Humphrey Murray,	1690
Thomas Fitzwater,	1690
Charles Pickering,	1690
Paul Saunders,	1690
Abraham Updegrave,	1690
[1691 wanting.]	
Samuel Richardson,	1692
John Holmes,	1692
William Salway,	1692
Lasse Cock,	1692
John White,	1692
Abraham Updegrave,	1692
Samuel Carpenter,	1693
Samuel Richardson,	1693
John White,	1693
James Fox,	1693
Samuel Richardson,	1694
Samuel Carpenter,	1694
Henry Waddy,	1694
James Fox,	1694
Edward Shippen, (Speaker,)	1695
Alexander Beardsley,	1695
James Fox,	1695
Robert Owen,	1695
John Bevan,	1695
John Parsons,	1695
Samuel Carpenter,	1696
Samuel Richardson,	1696
James Fox,	1696
Nicholas Waln,	1696
Samuel Richardson,	1697
James Fox,	1697
Robert Owen,	1697
Nicholas Waln,	1697
Anthony Morris,	1698
James Fox,	1698
Samuel Richardson,	1698
Andrew Bankson,	1698
Anthony Morris,	1699
James Fox,	1699
Isaac Norris,	1699
John Bevan,	1699
John Bevan,	1700
Anthony Morris,	1700

117

Nicholas Waln, ...	1700
Isaac Norris, ...	1700
Samuel Richardson, ...	1700
John Parsons, ...	1700
Edward Shippen. (extra session,)	1700
Griffith Owen, (extra session,)	1700
Rowland Ellis, (extra session,)	1700
Isaac Norris, (extra session,)	1700
Anthony Morris, ...	1701
Samuel Richardson, ...	1701
Nicholas Waln, ...	1701
Isaac Norris, ...	1701
David Lloyd, (Speaker,)	1702
Reese Thomas, ...	1702
Everard Bolton, ...	1702
Joseph Wilcox, ...	1702
Joshua Carpenter, ...	1702
Edmund Orpwood, ...	1704
John Roberts, ...	1704
Francis Rawle, ...	1704
Isaac Norris, ...	1705
Richard Hill, ...	1705
Rowland Ellis, ...	1705
Reese Thomas, ...	1705
Samuel Cart, ...	1705
John Goodson, ...	1705
William Carter, ...	1705
John Cook, ...	1705
David Lloyd, ...	1706
Joshua Carpenter, ...	1706
Robert Jones, ...	1706
John Roberts, ...	1706
Griffith Jones, ...	1706
Samuel Richardson, ...	1706
Joseph Wilcox, ...	1706
Francis Rawle, ...	1706
David Lloyd, (Speaker,)	1707
John Roberts, ...	1707
Griffith Jones, ...	1707
Francis Rawle, ...	1707
Joseph Wilcox, ...	1707
Robert Jones, ...	1707
Joshua Carpenter, ...	1707
Samuel Richardson, ...	1707
David Lloyd, (Speaker,)	1708
Joseph Wilcox, ...	1708

John Roberts,	1708
Francis Rawle,	1708
Joshua Carpenter,	1708
Griffith Jones,	1708
Francis Cooke,	1708
John Cooke,	1708
David Lloyd, (Speaker,)	1709
Joseph Wilcox,	1709
John Cooke,	1709
John Roberts,	1709
Griffith Jones,	1709
Francis Cooke,	1709
Samuel Richardson,	1709
Peter Rambo,	1709
Edward Farmer,	1710
William Trent,	1710
Edward Jones,	1710
Thomas Masters,	1710.
Thomas Jones,	1710
Samuel Cart,	1710
Jonathan Dickinson,	1710
David Giffing,	1710
Edward Farmer,	1711
Benjamin Duffield,	1711
Owen Roberts,	1711
David Lloyd,	1711
Isaac Norris,	1711
John Roberts,	1711
Robert Jones,	1711
Joseph Wilcox,	1711
Samuel Preston,	1712
Robert Jones,	1712
Isaac Norris, (Speaker,)	1712
Richard Hill,	1712
Edmund Orpwood,	1712
Benjamin Duffield,	1712
George Roach,	1712
Clement Plumsted,	1712
Edward Farmer,	1713
Robert Jones,	1713
Toby Leech,	1713
John Roberts,	1713
Thomas Rutter,	1713
Nicholas Waln,	1713
Matthias Keen,	1713
John Warner,	1713

Robert Jones, ... 1714
Jestell Jestis, ... 1714
Edward Farmer, ... 1714
John Warner, ... 1714
Nicholas Waln, ... 1714
Toby Leech, ... 1714
John Roberts, ... 1714
Thomas Rutter, ... 1714
John Roberts, ... 1715
Jestell Jestis, ... 1715
Robert Jones, ... 1715
Edward Farmer, ... 1715
Toby Leech, ... 1715
Nicholas Waln, ... 1715
John Warner, ... 1715
Benjamin Duffield, ... 1715
Richard Hill, (Speaker,) 1716
Isaac Norris, ... 1716
William Trent, ... 1716
Jonathan Dickinson, ... 1716
Thomas Masters, ... 1716
Joseph Redman, ... 1716
Clement Plumsted, ... 1716
William Fishbourne, ... 1716
Edward Farmer, ... 1717
Toby Leech, ... 1717
Thomas Paschall, ... 1717
Robert Jones, ... 1717
Joseph Wilcox, ... 1717
John Roberts, ... 1717
Lasse Bore, ... 1717
Nicholas Waln, ... 1717
Robert Jones, ... 1718
Edward Farmer, ... 1718
Richard Hill, ... 1718
William Fishbourne, ... 1718
Clement Plumsted, ... 1718
Morris Morris, ... 1718
Jonathan Dickinson, (Speaker,) 1718
Matthias Holstein, ... 1718
Richard Hill, ... 1719
William Trent, (Speaker,) 1719
Robert Jones, ... 1719
Jonathan Dickinson, ... 1719
William Fishbourne, ... 1719
Toby Leech, ... 1719

Rees Thomas, ... 1719
Francis Rawle, ... 1719
Robert Jones, ... 1720
Samuel Carpenter, ... 1720
Rees Thomas, ... 1720
Isaac Norris, (Speaker,) 1720
Morris Morris, ... 1720
Clement Plumsted, ... 1720
William Trent, ... 1720
Richard Hill, ... 1720
Robert Jones, ... 1721
Samuel Carpenter, Sr., ... 1721
Francis Rawle, ... 1721
Morris Morris, ... 1721
Benjamin Duffield, ... 1721
John Swift, ... 1721
William Tidmarsh, ... 1721
Benjamin Vining, ... 1721
Samuel Carpenter, ... 1722
Francis Rawle, ... 1722
Matthias Holstein, ... 1722
John Swift, ... 1722
Robert Jones, ... 1722
Anthony Morris, ... 1722
Hugh Evans, ... 1722
Benjamin Vining, ... 1722
Anthony Morris, ... 1723
Morris Morris, ... 1723
Matthias Holstein, ... 1723
John Swift, ... 1723
Francis Rawle, ... 1723
Benjamin Vining, ... 1723
Job Goodson, ... 1723
Samuel Hudson, ... 1723
Anthony Morris, ... 1724
Job Goodson, ... 1724
Morris Morris, ... 1724
Francis Rawle, ... 1724
John Swift, ... 1724
Samuel Hudson, ... 1724
Edward Farmer, ... 1724
Matthias Holstein, ... 1724
Evan Owen, ... 1725
Matthias Holstein, ... 1725
Francis Rawle, ... 1725
Anthony Rawle, ... 1725

John Swift, ...	1725
Job Goodson, ...	1725
Edward Farmer, ...	1725
Ludovic C. Sprogel, ...	1725
Edward Farmer, ...	1726
John Swift, ...	1726
Sir William Keith, ...	1726
Francis Rawle, (deceased.)	1726
Job Goodson,.	1726
Lodovic C. Sprogel, ...	1726
Edward Horne, ...	1726
Morris Morris, ...	1726
William Monington, (*vice* Rawle, deceased,) . . .	1727
Morris Morris, ...	1727
William Monington, ...	1727
Edward Horne, ...	1727
Sir William Keith, ...	1727
John Swift, ...	1727
Job Goodson, ...	1727
Ludovic C. Sprogel, ...	1727
Thomas Rutter, ...	1727
Edward Farmer, ...	1728
John Warder, ...	1728
William Monington, ... '.	1728
John Swift, ...	1728
Edward Horne, ...	1728
Thomas Rutter, ...	1728
David Potts, ...	1728
Ludovic C. Sprogel, ...	1728
Jonathan Robeson, ...	1729
Job Goodson, ...	1729
John Swift, ...	1729
William Monington, ...	1729
Edward Horne, ...	1729
David Potts, ...	1729
John Cadwalader, ...	1729
Thomas Rutter, Jr., ...	1729
Jonathan Robeson, ...	1730
William Monington, ...	1730
Thomas Leech, ...	1730
Job Goodson, ...	1730
John Cadwalader, ...	1730
William Allen, ...	1730
David Potts, (deceased,)	1730
John White, ...	1730
John Kinsey, (*vice* Potts, deceased,)	1730

122

William Allen,	1731
Jonathan Robeson,	1731
Thomas Leech,	1731
John Kinsey,	1731
John Cadwalader,	1731
William Monington,	1731
Job Goodson,	1731
Edward Farmer	1731
Jonathan Robeson,	1732
Thomas Leech,	1732
John Kinsey,	1732
William Allen,	1732
Robert Jones,	1732
Job Goodson,	1732
William Monington,	1732
John Cadwalader,	1732
Robert Jones,	1733
Jonathan Robeson,	1733
Job Goodson,	1733
Thomas Leech,	1733
John Kinsey,	1733
William Allen,	1733
John Cadwalader,	1733
William Monington,	1733
Robert Jones,	1734
Thomas Leech,	1734
William Monington,	1734
John Kinsey,	1734
Jonathan Robeson,	1734
William Allen,	1734
Job Goodson,	1734
Isaac Norris,	1734
Thomas Leech,	1735
Robert Jones,	1735
John Kinsey,	1735
Job Goodson,	1735
Edward Warner,	1735
William Allen,	1735
Isaac Norris,	1735
John Jones,	1735
Thomas Leech,	1736
John Kinsey,	1736
Robert Jones,	1736
Edward Warner,	1736
William Allen,	1736
Job Goodson,	1736

123

Jonathan Robeson, ... 1736
Septimus Robinson, ... 1736
Robert Jones, ... 1737
John Kinsey, ... 1737
Thomas Leech, ... 1737
Jonathan Robeson, ... 1737
Edward Warner, ... 1737
William Allen, ... 1737
Isaac Norris, ... 1737
William Monington, ... 1737
Edward Warner, ... 1738
William Monington, ... 1738
Thomas Leech, ... 1738
John Kinsey, ... 1738
William Allen, ... 1738
Job Goodson, ... 1738
Jonathan Robeson, ... 1738
Morris Morris, ... 1738
Robert Jones, ... 1739
Edward Warner, ... 1739
John Kinsey, (Speaker,) 1739
Isaac Norris, ... 1739
Owen Evans, ... 1739
Joseph Trotter, ... 1739
Thomas Leech, ... 1739
James Morris, ... 1739
Thomas Leech, ... 1740
John Kinsey, (Speaker,) 1740
Robert Jones, ... 1740
Isaac Norris, ... 1740
Edward Warner, ... 1740
Joseph Trotter, ... 1740
James Morris, ... 1740
Owen Evans, ... 1740
John Kinsey, ... 1741
Isaac Norris, ... 1741
Owen Evans, ... 1741
Robert Jones, ... 1741
Thomas Leech, ... 1741
Edward Warner, ... 1741
Joseph Trotter, ... 1741
James Morris, ... 1741
Thomas Leech, ... 1742
John Kinsey, (Speaker,) 1742
Robert Jones, ... 1742
Isaac Norris, ... 1742

Edward Warner,	1742
Owen Evans,	1742
James Morris,	1742
Joseph Trotter,	1742
John Kinsey, (Speaker,)	1743
Isaac Norris,	1743
Thomas Leech,	1743
Edward Warner,	1743
James Morris,	1743
Joseph Trotter,	1743
Owen Evans,	1743
Robert Jones,	1743
Isaac Norris,	1744
Thomas Leech,	1744
John Kinsey, (Speaker,)	1744
Robert Jones,	1744
Edward Warner,	1744
James Morris,	1744
Owen Evans,	1744
Joseph Trotter,	1744
John Kinsey,	1745
Isaac Norris,	1745
Edward Warner,	1745
Joseph Trotter,	1745
Thomas Leech,	1745
James Morris,	1745
Robert Jones,	1745
Owen Evans,	1745
John Kinsey, (Speaker,)	1746
Isaac Norris,	1746
Joseph Trotter,	1746
Thomas Leech,	1746
James Morris,	1746
Owen Evans,	1746
Edward Warner,	1746
Hugh Evans,	1746
John Kinsey, (Speaker,)	1747
Thomas Leech,	1747
Isaac Norris,	1747
Edward Warner,	1747
Joseph Trotter,	1747
James Morris,	1747
Owen Evans,	1747
Hugh Evans,	1747
John Kinsey, (Speaker,)	1748
Isaac Norris,	1748

Owen Evans, ... 1748
Hugh Evans, ... 1748
Edward Warner, ... 1748
Joseph Trotter, ... 1748
James Morris, ... 1748
Oswald Peele, ... 1748
John Kinsey, (Speaker,) 1749
Isaac Norris, ... 1749
Edward Warner, ... 1749
Joseph Trotter, ... 1749
James Morris, ... 1749
Oswald Peele, ... 1749
Owen Evans, ... 1749
Hugh Evans, ... 1749
Isaac Norris, (Speaker,) 1750
Edward Warner, ... 1750
Owen Evans, ... 1750
Hugh Evans, ... 1750
Joseph Trotter, ... 1750
Israel Pemberton, Jr., ... 1750
Evan Morgan, ... 1750
John Smith, ... 1750
Isaac Norris, (Speaker,) 1751
Edward Warner, ... 1751
Hugh Evans, ... 1751
Evan Morgan, ... 1751
Joseph Trotter, ... 1751
John Smith, ... 1751
Joshua Morris, ... 1751
Henry Pawling, ... 1751
Isaac Norris, (Speaker,) 1752
Edward Warner, ... 1752
Joseph Trotter, ... 1752
Evan Morgan, ... 1752
Hugh Evans, ... 1752
Joshua Morris, ... 1752
John Smith, ... 1752
Joseph Stretch, ... 1752
Isaac Norris, (Speaker,) 1753
Edward Warner, ... 1753
Evan Morgan, ... 1753
Joseph Trotter, ... 1753
Joshua Morris, ... 1753
Hugh Evans, ... 1753
Joseph Stretch, ... 1753
Joseph Fox, ... 1753

Isaac Norris, (Speaker,) 1754
Evan Morgan, ... 1754
Hugh Evans, ... 1754
Joseph Stretch, ... 1754
Edward Warner, ... 1754
Joseph Fox, ... 1754
Joshua Morris, ... 1754
Joseph Trotter, ... 1754
Isaac Norris, (Speaker,) 1755
Joseph Trotter, ... 1755
James Pemberton, ... 1755
Joseph Stretch, ... 1755
Joseph Fox, ... 1755
Joshua Morris, ... 1755
Richard Pearne, ... 1755
John Hughes, ... 1755
Isaac Norris, (Speaker,) 1756
Joseph Fox, ... 1756
Thomas Leech, ... 1756
Daniel Roberdeau, ... 1756
John Hughes, ... 1756
John Baynton, ... 1756
Joseph Galloway, ... 1756
Richard Pearne, ... 1756
Isaac Norris, (Speaker,) 1757
Joseph Fox, ... 1757
Thomas Leech, ... 1757
John Hughes, ... , . 1757
John Baynton, ... 1757
Daniel Roberdeau, ... : . 1757
Joseph Galloway, ... 1757
Richard Pearne, ... 1757
Isaac Norris, (Speaker,) 1758
Thomas Leech, ... 1758
Joseph Galloway, ... 1758
John Baynton, ... 1758
Daniel Roberdeau, ... 1758
John Hughes, ... 1758
Richard Pearne, ... 1758
Joseph Fox, ... 1758
Joseph Galloway, ... 1759
Joseph Fox, ... 1759
John Baynton, ... 1759
John Hughes, ... 1759
Daniel Roberdeau, ... 1759
Richard Pearne, ... 1759

Isaac Norris, (Speaker,)	1759
Thomas Leech,	1759
Isaac Norris, (Speaker,)	1760
Thomas Leech,	1760
Joseph Fox,	1760
Joseph Galloway,	1760
Richard Pearne,	1760
John Hughes,	1760
Daniel Roberdeau,	1760
John Baynton,	1760
Isaac Norris, (Speaker,)	1761
Thomas Leech,	1761
John Hughes,	1761
Joseph Galloway,	1761
John Baynton,	1761
Joseph Fox,	1761
Edward Penington,	1761
Rowland Evans,	1761
Isaac Norris, (Speaker,)	1762
Joseph Fox,	1762
John Hughes,	1762
Rowland Evans,	1762
Plunket Fleeson,	1762
John Dickinson,	1762
Joseph Galloway,	1762
Jonathan Mifflin,	1762
Isaac Norris, (Speaker,)	1763
Joseph Fox,	1763
Joseph Galloway,	1763
John Hughes,	1763
Rowland Evans,	1763
John Dickinson,	1763
Plunket Fleeson,	1763
Joseph Richardson,	1763
Isaac Norris, (Speaker,)	1764
Joseph Richardson,	1764
John Dickinson,	1764
Henry Pawling,	1764
Joseph Fox,	1764
Amos Strettell,	1764
Henry Kepple,	1764
John Hughes,	1765
Isaac Norris,	1765
Joseph Fox, (Speaker,)	1765
Joseph Richardson,	1765
Henry Pawling,	1765

Rowland Evans,	1765
Thomas Livezey,	1765
Michael Hillegas,	1765
Joseph Galloway,	1765
Joseph Richardson,	1766
Henry Pawling,	1766
Rowland Evans,	1766
Thomas Livezey,	1766
John Potts,	1766
Joseph Fox,	1766
Michael Hillegas,	1766
Joseph Galloway, (Speaker,)	1766
Rowland Evans,	1767
Joseph Galloway, (Speaker,)	1767
Henry Pawling,	1767
Joseph Richardson,	1767
Michael Hillegas,	1767
Thomas Livezey,	1767
Samuel Potts,	1767
Joseph Fox,	1767
Joseph Galloway, (Speaker,)	1768
Joseph Fox,	1768
Joseph Richardson,	1768
Michael Hillegas,	1768
Henry Pawling,	1768
Rowland Evans,	1768
Thomas Livezey,	1768
Samuel Potts,	1768
Rowland Evans,	1769
Henry Pawling,	1769
Michael Hillegas,	1769
Thomas Livezey,	1769
Joseph Fox,	1769
Samuel Potts,	1769
Joseph Galloway, (Speaker,)	1769
Joseph Richardson,	1769
Michael Hillegas,	1770
Rowland Evans,	1770
Henry Pawling,	1770
Joseph Fox,	1770
Israel Jacobs,	1770
Thomas Livezey,	1770
Joseph Parker,	1770
Samuel Rhoads,	1770
Michael Hillegas,	1771
Henry Pawling,	1771

Joseph Parker,	1771
Israel Jacobs,	1771
Joseph Fox,	1771
Samuel Rhoads,	1771
Thomas Livezey,	1771
Rowland Evans,	1771
Israel Jacobs,	1772
Henry Pawling,	1772
Jonathan Roberts,	1772
Michael Hillegas,	1772
Samuel Rhoads,	1772
Joseph King,	1772
Joseph Parker,	1772
George Gray,	1772
Henry Pawling,	1773
Michael Hillegas,	1773
Joseph Parker,	1773
Israel Jacobs,	1773
George Gray,	1773
Samuel Rhoads,	1773
Jonathan Roberts,	1773
Samuel Miles,	1773
George Gray,	1774
Henry Pawling,	1774
John Dickinson,	1774
Joseph Parker,	1774
Israel Jacobs,	1774
Jonathan Roberts,	1774
Michael Hillegas,	1774
Samuel Rhoads,	1774
John Dickinson,	1775
Michael Hillegas,	1775
George Gray,	1775
Thomas Potts,	1775
Samuel Miles,	1775
Joseph Parker,	1775
Robert Morris,	1775
Jonathan Roberts,	1775

Mayors.

Edward Shippen,		1701
Anthony Morris,	Oct.	12, 1703
Griffith Jones,	Oct.	4, 1704
Joseph Wilcox,	Oct.	2, 1705
Nathan Stanbury,	Oct.	1, 1706
Thomas Masters,	Oct.	7, 1707–8

130

Richard Hill, ... Oct. 4, 1709
William Carter, ... Oct. —, 1710
Samuel Preston, ... Oct. 2, 1711
Jonathan Dickinson, ... Oct. 7, 1712
George Roach, ... Oct. 6, 1713
Richard Hill, . Oct. 5, 1714; Oct. 4, 1715; Oct. 2, 1716
Jonathan Dickinson, . . . Oct. 8, 1717; Oct. 7, 1718
William Fishbourne, ... Oct. —, 1719
William Fishbourne, . . . Oct. 4, 1720; Oct. 3, 1721
James Logan, ... Oct. 2, 1722
Clement Plumsted, ... Oct. 1, 1723
Isaac Norris, ... Oct. 6, 1724
William Hudson, ... Oct. 5, 1725
Charles Read, ... Oct. —, 1726
Thomas Lawrence, ... Oct. 3, 1727; Oct. 2, 1728
Thomas Griffitts, ... Oct. 7, 1729; Oct. 6, 1730
Samuel Hasell, ... Oct. 6, 1731; Oct. 3, 1732
Thomas Griffitts, ... Oct. 2, 1733
Thomas Lawrence, ... Oct. 1, 1734
William Allen, ... Oct. 7, 1735
Clement Plumsted, ... Oct. 5, 1736
Thomas Griffitts, ... Oct. 4, 1737
Anthony Morris, ... Oct. 3, 1738
Edward Roberts, ... Oct. 2, 1739
Samuel Hasell, ... Oct. 7, 1740
Clement Plumsted, ... Oct. 6, 1741
William Till, ... Oct. 5, 1742
Benjamin Shoemaker, ... Oct. 4, 1743
Edward Shippen, ... Oct. 2, 1744
James Hamilton, ... Oct. 1, 1745
William Atwood, ... Oct. 7, 1746; Oct. 9, 1747
Charles Willing, ... Oct. 4, 1748
Thomas Lawrence, ... Oct. 3, 1749
William Plumsted, ... Oct. 2, 1750
Robert Strettell, ... Oct. 1, 1751
Benjamin Shoemaker, ... Oct. 3, 1752
Thomas Lawrence, ... Oct. 2, 1753
Charles Willing, (*vice* Thomas Law-
   rence, deceased,) . . . Apr. 25, 1754; Oct. 1, 1754
William Plumsted, (*vice* Charles Wil-
   ling, deceased,) . . . . Dec. 4, 1754; Oct. 7, 1755
Atwood Shute, ... Oct. 5, 1756
Atwood Shute, ... Oct. 4, 1757
Thomas Lawrence, ... Oct. 15, 1758
John Stamper, ... Oct. 2, 1759
Benjamin Shoemaker, ... Oct. 7, 1760

131

Jacob Duché, ...		Oct.	6, 1761
Henry Harrison, ...		Oct.	5, 1762
Thomas Willing, ...		Oct.	4, 1763
Thomas Lawrence, ...		Oct.	4, 1764
John Lawrence, ...	Oct. 1, 1765 ;	Oct.	7, 1766
Isaac Jones, ...	Oct. 6, 1767 ;	Oct.	4, 1768
Samuel Shoemaker, . . .	Oct. 3, 1769 ;	Oct.	2, 1770
John Gibson, ...	Oct. 1, 1771 ;	Oct.	6, 1772
William Fisher, ...		Oct.	5, 1773
Samuel Rhoads, ...		Oct.	4, 1774
Samuel Powel, ...		Oct.	3, 1775

Common Councilmen.

John Parsons, ...			1701
William Lee, ...			1701
Thomas Paschall, ...			1701
Edward Smout, ...			1701
James Atkinson, ...			1701
Francis Cooke, ...			1701
William Hudson, ...			1701
Nehemiah Allen, ...			1701
John Budd, Jr., ...			1701
Samuel Buckley, ...			1701
Pentecost Teague, ...			1701
Henry Badcock, ...			1701
John Parsons, attending as member, . . .		Oct.	3, 1704
William Hudson, do. . .		Oct.	3, 1704
William Lee, do. . . .		Oct.	3, 1704
John Budd, Jr., do. . .		Oct.	3, 1704
Edward Smout, do. . . .		Oct.	3, 1704
James Atkinson, do. . .		Oct.	3, 1704
Penticost Teague, do. . . .		Oct.	3, 1704
Francis Cook, do. . .		Oct.	3, 1704
Henry Badcock, do. . . .		Oct.	3, 1704
Robert Yeildall, do. . .		Oct.	3, 1704
Joseph Yard, do. . . .		Oct.	3, 1704
Thomas Griffith, do. . .		Oct.	3, 1704
John Redman, Sen., do. . . .		Oct.	3, 1704
Thomas Paschall, attending		Dec.	15, 1704
Nehemiah Allen, do.		Sept.	29, 1705
Joshua Carpenter, elected, ...		Oct.	2, 1705
Abraham Bickley, elected, ...		Oct.	2, 1705
Thomas Bradford, elected, ...		Oct.	2, 1705
John Webb, elected, ...		Oct.	2, 1705
Samuel Hall, ...		Oct.	7, 1707
John McComb, ...		Oct.	7, 1707

Henry Flower,	Oct.	5, 1708
Peter Stretch,	Oct.	5, 1708
David Griffin,	Oct.	5, 1708
George Claypoole,	Oct.	5, 1708
Owen Roberts,	Oct.	2, 1711
Clement Plumsted,	Oct.	7, 1712
George Falconer,	Oct.	7, 1712
John Jones Boller,	Oct.	7, 1712
Nathaniel Edgcomb,	Oct.	7, 1712
Joseph Redman,	Oct.	6, 1713
John Warder,	Oct.	6, 1713
John Vanlear,	Oct.	6, 1713
George Claypoole,	Oct.	6, 1713
William Fishbourne,	Oct.	6, 1713
Thomas Warton,	Oct.	6, 1713
Anthony Morris, Jr.,	Oct.	4, 1715
Daniel Ridley,	Oct.	4, 1715
Thomas Redman,	Oct.	4, 1715
James Parrock,	Oct.	2, 1716
Samuel Carpenter,	Oct.	2, 1716
Richard Moore,	Oct.	2, 1716
Charles Read,	Oct.	2, 1716
Samuel Powell,	Oct.	1, 1717
Edward Roberts,	Oct.	1, 1717
Evan Owen,	Oct.	1, 1717
George Fitzwater,	Oct.	1, 1717
Israel Pemberton,	Oct.	7, 1718
John Carpenter,	Oct.	7, 1718
John Cadwalader,	Oct.	7, 1718
Joseph Buckley,	Oct.	7, 1718
Thomas Griffitts,	Oct.	7, 1718
Thomas Tresse,	Oct.	7, 1718
Thomas Lawrence,	Oct.	3, 1722
George Calvert,	Oct.	3, 1722
Edward Owen,	Oct.	3, 1722
George McCall,	Oct.	3, 1722
Robert Ellis,	Oct.	3, 1722
Ralph Assheton,	Oct.	6, 1724
William Allen,	Oct.	3, 1727
Thomas Masters,	Oct.	3, 1727
Andrew Bradford,	Oct.	3, 1727
Isaac Norris, Jr.,	Oct.	3, 1727
Alexander Woodrop,	Oct.	3, 1727
Henry Hodge,	Oct.	3, 1727
Samuel Hasell,	Oct.	2, 1728
Thomas Chase,	Oct.	2, 1728

Peter Lloyd,	Oct.	7, 1729
Samuel Powell,	Oct.	7, 1729
William Attwood,	Oct.	7, 1729
Joseph Turner,.	Oct.	7, 1729
James Steel,	Oct.	6, 1730
George Emlen,	Oct.	6, 1730
Abram Taylor,	Oct.	6, 1730
Samuel Powell, Jr.,	Oct.	6, 1730
George Mifflin,	Oct.	6, 1730
John White,	Oct.	6, 1730
Samuel Mickel,	Oct.	3, 1732
Edward Shippen,	Oct.	3, 1732
George House,	Oct.	3, 1732
John Dilwyn,	Oct.	3, 1732
Benjamin Shoemaker,	Oct.	3, 1732
Joseph England,	Oct.	3, 1732
James Bingham,	Oct.	3, 1732
Joseph Paschall,	Oct.	3, 1732
William Till,	Oct.	2, 1739
Joshua Maddox,	Oct.	2, 1739
Nathaniel Allen,	Oct.	2, 1739
William Coleman,	Oct.	2, 1739
James Hamilton,.	Oct.	2, 1739
William Plumsted,	Oct.	2, 1739
Robert Strettell,	Oct.	6, 1741
William Parsons,	Oct.	6, 1741
Andrew Hamilton,	Oct.	6, 1741
Samuel Rhoades,	Oct.	6, 1741
Thomas Hopkinson,	Oct.	6, 1741
Joseph Morris,.	Oct.	5, 1742
Joseph Shippen,	Oct.	5, 1742
Joshua Emlen,	Oct.	5, 1742
Richard Nixon,	Oct.	5, 1742
Samuel Austen,	Oct.	5, 1742
Isaac Tones,.	Oct.	5, 1742
William Logan,	Oct.	4, 1743
Charles Willing,	Oct.	4, 1743
Attwood Shute,	Oct.	4, 1743
Septimus Robinson,	Oct.	4, 1743
Alexander Graydon,	Oct.	1, 1745
John Inglis,	Oct.	1, 1745
Richard Stanley,	Oct.	1, 1745
William Shippen,.	Oct.	1, 1745
Thomas Bond,.	Oct.	1, 1745
William Biddle,	Oct.	1, 1745
John Mifflin,	Oct.	6, 1747

John Stamper,	Oct.	6, 1747
John Sober,	Oct.	6, 1747
Tench Francis,	Oct.	6, 1747
John Wilcocks,	Oct.	6, 1747
Samuel McCall, Jr.,	Oct.	6, 1747
Phineas Bond,	Oct.	6, 1747
Joseph Sims,	Oct.	6, 1747
Benjamin Franklin,	Oct.	4, 1748
Thomas Lawrence, Jr.,	Oct.	4, 1748
Thomas Cadwalader,	Oct.	1, 1751
William Coxe,	Oct.	1, 1751
Lloyd Zachary,	Oct.	1, 1751
Charles Norris,	Oct.	1, 1751
John Redman,	Oct.	1, 1751
William Humphreys,	Oct.	1, 1751
Samuel Smith,	Oct.	1, 1751
Amos Strettell,	Oct.	1, 1751
William Bingham,	Oct.	1, 1751
Edward Shippen, Jr.,	Oct.	7, 1755
Samuel Mifflin,	Oct.	7, 1755
Alexander Huston,	Oct.	7, 1755
John Wallace,	Oct.	7, 1755
Alexander Stedman,	Oct.	7, 1755
Andrew Elliot,	Oct.	7, 1755
Samuel Morris,	Oct.	7, 1755
Jacob Duché,	Oct.	7, 1755
Samuel Shoemaker,	Oct.	7, 1755
Thomas Willing,	Oct.	7, 1755
Henry Harrison,	Oct.	4, 1757
Daniel Benezet,	Oct.	4, 1757
Charles Stedman,	Oct.	4, 1757
William Rush,	Oct.	4, 1757
John Swift,	Oct.	4, 1757
Townsend White,	Oct.	4, 1757
William Vanderspiegel,	Oct.	4, 1757
Joseph Wood,	Oct.	4, 1757
John Allen,	Oct.	5, 1762
John Lawrence,	Oct.	5, 1762
Redmond Conyngham,	Oct.	5, 1762
Evan Morgan,	Oct.	5, 1762
John Gibson,	Oct.	5, 1762
James Tilghman,	Oct.	2, 1764
Archibald McCall,	Oct.	2, 1764
Andrew Allen,	Oct.	6, 1767
James Allen,	Oct.	6, 1767
Joshua Howell,	Oct.	6, 1767

Joseph Swift,	Oct.	6, 1767
William Fisher,	Oct.	6, 1767
William Parr,	Oct.	6, 1767
John Wilcocks,	Oct.	6, 1767
George Clymer,	Oct.	6, 1767
Joseph Shippen, Jr.,	Oct.	2, 1770
John Cadwalader.	Oct.	2, 1770
Samuel Powel,	Oct.	2, 1770
Alexander Wilcocks,	Oct.	2, 1770
Stephen Carmick,	Oct.	2, 1770
Peter Chevalier,	Oct.	2, 1770
John Potts,	Oct.	4, 1774
Samuel Meredith,	Oct.	4, 1774
James Biddle,	Oct.	4, 1774
Samuel Howell,	Oct.	4, 1774
Isaac Cox,	Oct.	4, 1774
Thomas Barclay,	Oct.	4, 1774

Aldermen.

Joshua Carpenter,		1701
Griffith Jones,		1701
Anthony Morris,		1701
Joseph Wilcox,		1701
Nathan Stanbury,		1701
Charles Read,		1701
Thomas Masters,		1701
William Carter,		1701
Joseph Wilcox,		1704
Jonathan Dickinson,		1716
Thomas Masters,		1716
Abraham Bickley,		1716
Joseph Turner,		1742-3
Edward Shippen,	Oct.	3, 1704
Griffith Jones,	Oct.	3, 1704
Joseph Wilcox,	Oct.	3, 1704
Nathan Stanbury,	Oct.	3, 1704
Charles Read,	Oct.	3, 1704
Thomas Masters,	Oct.	3, 1704
William Carter,	Oct.	3, 1704
John Jones,	Oct.	3, 1704
Joshua Carpenter,	Oct.	3, 1704
Edward Smout,	Oct.	3, 1704
Thomas Story,	Oct.	3, 1704
Anthony Morris,	Oct.	3, 1704
Samuel Richardson,	Oct.	2, 1705
George Roach,	Oct.	5, 1708

Richard Hill,	Oct.	5, 1708
Samuel Preston,	Oct.	5, 1708
Isaac Norris,	Oct.	5, 1708
Jonathan Dickinson,	Oct.	2, 1711
George Roach,	Oct.	7, 1712
Joseph Growdon,	Oct.	6, 1713
Isaac Norris,	Oct.	6, 1713
Pentecost Teague,	Oct.	6, 1713
William Hudson,	Oct.	4, 1715
Abraham Bickley,	Oct.	4, 1715
Joseph Redman,	Oct.	4, 1715
James Logan,	Oct.	1, 1717
Thomas Griffitts,	Oct.	7, 1718
William Fishbourne,	Oct.	7, 1718
Clement Plumsted,	Oct.	4, 1720
Israel Pemberton,	Oct.	4, 1720
Clement Plumsted,	Oct.	2, 1722
Israel Pemberton,	Oct.	2, 1722
Thomas Griffitts,	Oct.	2, 1722
Charles Read,	Oct.	2, 1722
Benj. Vining,	Oct.	2, 1722
Anthony Morris,	Sept.	29, 1726
Edward Roberts,	Oct.	3, 1727
Samuel Hasell,	Oct.	7, 1729
John Jones,	Oct.	7, 1729
George Fitzwater,	Oct.	7, 1729
George Claypoole,	Oct.	7, 1729
William Allen,	Oct.	6, 1730
Isaac Norris, Jr.,	Oct.	6, 1730
Israel Pemberton,	Oct.	2, 1733
Anthony Morris,	Oct.	2, 1733
Benjamin Shoemaker,	Oct.	6, 1741
William Till,	Oct.	6, 1741
Joseph Turner,	Oct.	6, 1741
James Hamilton,	Oct.	6, 1741
William Atwood,	Oct.	4, 1743
Abram Taylor,	Oct.	4, 1743
Samuel Powel, Jr.,	Oct.	4, 1743
Edward Shippen,	Oct.	4, 1743
Robert Strettell,	Nov.	16, 1748
Benjamin Franklin,	Oct.	1, 1751
John Mifflin,	Oct.	1, 1751
John Stamper,	Oct.	7, 1755
Attwood Shute,	Oct.	7, 1755
Thomas Lawrence,	Oct.	7, 1755
Alexander Stedman,	Oct.	5, 1756

Samuel Mifflin,	Oct.	5, 1756
John Wilcocks,	Oct.	4, 1757
Jacob Duché,	Oct.	4, 1757
William Coxe,	Oct.	4, 1757
Thomas Willing,	Oct.	2, 1759
Daniel Benezet,	Oct.	2, 1759
Henry Harrison,	Oct.	6, 1761
Samuel Rhoads,	Oct.	6, 1761
Isaac Jones,	Oct.	2, 1764
John Lawrence,	Oct.	2, 1764
Amos Strettell,	Oct.	7, 1766
Samuel Shoemaker,	Oct.	7, 1766
John Gibson,	Oct.	6, 1767
James Allen,	Oct.	2, 1770
Joshua Howell,	Oct.	2, 1770
William Fisher,	Oct.	2, 1770
Samuel Powell,	Oct.	4, 1774
George Clymer,	Oct.	4, 1774

Wardens of the Port of Philadelphia.

Peter Reeve,	1767
Michael Hulings,	1767
John Nixon,	1767
Abel James,	1767
Robert Morris,	1767
Thomas Penrose,	1767

Measurers of Corn and Salt Exported and Imported.

Nehemiah Allen,	1734
John Nolson,	1774

Barrack Masters.

Joseph Fox,	1767 to 1776
Lewis Nicola,	Since March, 1776

Inspectors of Flour.

Joseph King,	1750
Thomas Pryor,	1774

Inspector of Beef and Pork.

Jonathan Evans,	1774

Collectors of Excise.

Charles Read,	1725–1733
John Hyatt,	1733–1737

Joseph Wharton, ... 1738–1744
Charles Read, ... 1735
Reese Meredith, ... 1742 (late 1745)
Judah Foulke, ... 1745–1750
Joseph Redman, ... 1751–1756
Joseph Stretch, (deceased,) . . . . . 1757 to 1771
William Crispin, ... 1771 to 1776

Regulator of Weights and Measures.

John Parker, ... July   21, 1707

City Treasurer.

William Fishbourne, ... Aug.   10, 1716

Special Commission to Notaries as Justices of the Peace.

James Humphreys, ... April   27, 1772
Matthew Clarkson, ... April   27, 1772
Peter Miller, ... April   27, 1772
John Ord. . . . . April   27, 1772

Justices for Trial of Negroes.

William Plumsted, ... Oct.   28, 1762
William Parr, ... Oct.   28, 1762
George Bryan, ... Sept.   25, 1766
James Biddle, ... Sept.   25, 1766
George Bryan, ... July   27, 1773
James Biddle, ... July   27, 1773

Land Waiter and Searcher of His Majesty's Customs.

John Hare, ... 1735
John Nelson, ... 1745
O'Sullivan Sutherland, ... 1766
William Sheppard, ... 1768
——— Smith, ... Aug.   27, 1770
George Drummond. 1770

Surveyor of Rates, Duties, and Impositions on Delaware Bay.

Joseph Shippen, ... 1761

Tide Surveyor at Port of Philadelphia.

——— Ross, dismissed, ... 1770
Arodi Thayer, ... 1771

Marshal and Sergeant-at-Mace of the Vice Admiralty.

Arodi Thayer, ... Sept.   7, 1770

Deputy Marshal and Serjeant-at-Mace of the Court of Vice Admiralty, having jurisdiction in New York, New Jersey, Pennsylvania, the lower counties on Delaware, Maryland, and Virginia.

John Smith, ... Feb. 1, 1771

Deputy Register and Clerk of Vice Admiralty at Philadelphia, jurisdiction as above.

John Smith, ... Feb. 10, 1773

Comptroller of Customs.

William Bully, ... 1727–28
Alexander Barclay, ... 1749–71
Lynford Lardner, *vice* Barclay, deceased, . . Jan. 15, 1771
Joshua Loring, Jr., ... Mar. 7, 1771
Zachariah Hood, ... April 15, 1773

Naval Officers of the Port of Philadelphia.

Robert Assheton, ... 1717
Thomas Græme, *vice* Assheton, deceased, . . 1727–1740–1761
Richard Hockley, ... 1772

Agents to Receive and Collect the Perquisites and Rights of Admiralty.

Isaac Miranda, ... 1727
Robert Charles, ... 1731–34
Sergeant Smythies, ... Oct. 11, 1734

Assembly.

Thomas Masters, ... 1704
Charles Read, ... 1704
David Lloyd, ... 1705
Edward Shippen, Sen., ... 1705
Francis Cooke, ... 1706
William Hudson, ... 1706
Francis Cooke, ... 1707
William Lee, ... 1707
Abraham Bickley, ... 1708
William Lee, ... 1708
Pentecost Teague, ... 1709
Abraham Bickley, ... 1709
Richard Hill, (Speaker,) 1710
Isaac Norris, ... 1710
Richard Hill, (Speaker,) 1711
Samuel Preston, ... 1711
Jonathan Dickinson, ... 1712
Thomas Masters, ... 1712

Isaac Norris,	1713
Richard Hill,	1713
Richard Hill,	1714
Samuel Preston, (refused to serve,)	1714
Clement Plumsted, (*vice* Preston,)	1715
Richard Hill,	1715
Isaac Norris,	1715
George Roach,	1716
Benjamin Vining,	1716
William Trent, (Speaker,)	1717
Abraham Bickley,	1717
Israel Pemberton,	1718
Isaac Norris,	1718
Isaac Norris,	1719
Clement Plumsted,	1719
William Fishbourne,	1720
Jonathan Dickinson,	1720
Joshua Carpenter,	1721
Anthony Morris,	1721
John Kearsley,	1722
Charles Read,	1722
John Kearsley,	1723
Thomas Redman,	1723
John Kearsley,	1724
Thomas Tresse,	1724
John Kearsley,	1725
Thomas Tresse,	1725
John Kearsley,	1726
Thomas Tresse,	1726
Thomas Tresse,	1727
John Kearsley,	1727
John Kearsley,	1728
Thomas Tresse,	1728
John Kearsley,	1729
Thomas Tresse,	1729
John Kearsley,	1730
Thomas Tresse,	1730
John Kearsley, (Burgess,)	1731
Israel Pemberton, (Burgess,)	1731
John Kearsley, (Burgess,)	1732
Israel Pemberton, (Burgess,)	1732
John Kearsley, (Burgess,)	1733
Israel Pemberton, (Burgess,)	1733
Israel Pemberton, (Burgess,)	1734
John Kearsley, (Burgess,)	1734
John Kearsley, (Burgess,)	1735

141

Israel Pemberton, (Burgess,) 1735
John Kearsley, (Burgess,) 1736
Israel Pemberton, (Burgess,) 1736
Israel Pemberton, (Burgess,) 1737
John Kearsley, (Burgess,) 1737
John Kearsley, (Burgess,) 1738
Israel Pemberton, (Burgess,) 1738
John Kearsley, (Burgess,) 1739
Israel Pemberton, (Burgess,) 1739
Israel Pemberton, (Burgess,) 1740
John Kearsley, (Burgess,) 1740
Israel Pemberton, (Burgess,) 1741
Oswald Peele, (Burgess,) 1741
Israel Pemberton, (Burgess,) 1742
Oswald Peele, (Burgess,) 1742
Israel Pemberton, (Burgess,) 1743
Oswald Peele, (Burgess,) 1743
Israel Pemberton, ... 1744
Oswald Peele, ... 1744
Israel Pemberton, (burgess,) 1745
Oswald Peele, (burgess,) 1745
Israel Pemberton, (burgess,) 1746
Oswald Peele, (burgess,) 1746
Oswald Peele, (burgess,) 1747
Israel Pemberton, (burgess,) 1747
Israel Pemberton, (burgess,) 1748
Thomas Leech, (burgess,) 1748
Israel Pemberton, (burgess,) 1749
Thomas Leech, (burgess,) 1749
Joseph Fox, (burgess,) 1750
William Clymer, (burgess,) 1750
Benjamin Franklin, (burgess,) 1751
Hugh Roberts, (burgess,) 1751
Benjamin Franklin, ... 1752
Hugh Roberts, ... 1752
Benjamin Franklin, ... 1753
William Callender, ... 1753
Benjamin Franklin, ... 1754
William Callender, ... 1754
Benjamin Franklin, ... 1755
William Callender, ... 1755
Benjamin Franklin, ... 1756
William Masters, ... 1756
William Masters, ... 1757
Benjamin Franklin, ... 1757
Benjamin Franklin, ... 1758

William Masters,	1758
Benjamin Franklin,	1759
William Masters,	1759
Benjamin Franklin,	1760
William Masters, (deceased,)	1760
Samuel Rhoads, (*vice* Masters, deceased,)	1761
Benjamin Franklin,	1761
Samuel Rhoads,	1761
Benjamin Franklin,	1762
Samuel Rhoads,	1762
Benjamin Franklin, (Speaker, May, 1764, for ballance of session,)	1763
Samuel Rhoads,	1763
Thomas Willing,	1764
George Bryan,	1764
Thomas Willing,	1765
James Pemberton,	1765
James Pemberton,	1766
John Ross,	1766
James Pemberton,	1767
John Ross,	1767
James Pemberton,	1768
John Ross,	1768
James Pemberton,	1769
John Ross,	1769
John Dickinson,	1770
Abel James,	1770
Samuel Shoemaker,	1771
Abel James,	1771
Samuel Shoemaker,	1772
Thomas Mifflin,	1772
Thomas Mifflin,	1773
Benjamin Franklin,	1773
Thomas Mifflin,	1774
Charles Thomson,	1774
Benjamin Franklin, (resigned,)	1775
Thomas Mifflin,	1775
David Rittenhouse, (*vice* Franklin resigned,)	1776
Samuel Howell, (additional balance of year,)	1776
George Clymer, (additional balance of year,)	1776
Andrew Allen, (additional balance of year,)	1776
Alexander Wilcocks, (additional balance of year,)	1776

OFFICERS FOR BUCKS COUNTY.

Sheriffs.

Richard Noble, ...	1682
Nicholas Waln, ...	May 4, 1685
Abraham Worley, ...	May 6, 1686
William Yardley, ...	Feb. 11, 1690
Israel Taylor, ...	Apr. 29, 1693
William Biles, Jr., ...	Dec. 27, 1704
William Croasdell, ...	Oct. 14, 1707
John Hall, ...	Oct. 3, 1717–18
Abraham de Normandie, ...	Oct. 3, 1719
John Hall, ...	Oct. 4, 1720–21
Thomas Biles, ...	Oct. 4, 1726–27
Timothy Smith, ...	Oct. 3, 1728–29–30
Isaac Penington, ...	Oct. 4, 1731–32
John Hall, ...	Oct. 4, 1733
Timothy Smith, ...	Oct. 4, 1734–35–36
John Hart, ...	Oct. 4, 1737–38–39
Joseph Jackson, ...	Oct. 3, 1740–41–42
John Hart, ...	Oct. 4, 1743–44–45
Amos Strickland, ...	Oct. 4, 1746–47–48
John Hart, ...	Oct. 8, 1749
Joseph Hart, ...	Oct. 3, 1750–51
William Yardley, ...	Oct. 4, 1752–53–54
Benjamin Chapman, ...	Oct. 4, 1755–56
Joseph Thornton, ...	Oct. 4, 1759–60–61
John Gregg, ...	Oct. 4, 1762–63–64
William Buckman, ...	Oct. 4, 1765–66–67
Joseph Ellicott, ...	Oct. 4, 1768–69–70
Richard Gibbs, ...	Oct. 5, 1771–72
Samuel Biles, ...	Oct. 4, 1773–74–75

Under Sheriff.

James Moon, ...	1714

Coroners.

Robert Hall, ...	Sept. 16, 1685
George White, ...	July 25, 1688
William Biles, ...	Oct. 3, 1717
John Cutler, ...	Oct. 3, 1718–19
Jeffrey Pollard, ...	Oct. 4, 1720
William Atkinson, ...	Oct. 4, 1721
Jonathan Woolston, ...	Oct. 4, 1726–30
William Atkinson, ...	Oct. 4, 1731–35

John Woolston, ...	Oct.	4, 1736
William Atkinson, ...	Oct.	4, 1737–40
John Hart, ...	Oct.	4, 1742
Joseph Chapman, ...	Oct.	4, 1743–45
John Chapman, ...	Oct.	4, 1746–47
John Hart, ...	Oct.	4, 1748
William Smith, ...	Oct.	8, 1749–51
Evan Jones, ...	Oct.	4, 1752–54
Simon Butler, ...	Oct.	4, 1755
William Ashburn, ...	Oct.	4, 1756–59
William Buckman, ...	Oct.	3, 1760–63
John Addis, ...	Oct.	4, 1764
William Doyle, ...	Oct.	4, 1765–67
James Wallace, ...	Oct.	4, 1768–72
George Fell, ...	Oct.	4, 1773–75

Sealer of Weights and Measures.

Thomas Watson, ...	Sept.	24, 1731

Clerk.

Robert Cole, ...	March	13, 1693

Prothonotary, Register and Recorder.

William Hicks, ...	April	5, 1770
Isaac Hicks, ...	June	6, 1772

Clerk of the Peace and General Quarter Sessions.

Isaac Hicks, ...	June	19, 1772

Surveyor.

Arthur Cook, ...	Sept.	19, 1686
Thomas Janney, ...	Sept.	19, 1686
Robert Longshore, ...		1693

Collectors of Money Granted Proprietary.

Edward Mayes, ...	March	28, 1704
Claus Johnson, ...	March	28, 1704
William Biles, ...	March	28, 1704
Thomas Stackhouse, ...	March	28, 1704

Collectors of Excise.

Thomas Clifford, (late Collector,)	1724
Nathan Watson, ...	1731–32–33
John Hall, ...	1735–36–37
William Atkinson, (deceased,)	1738–49
John Hall, (vice William Atkinson, deceased,) . .	1749–50

John Woolston,	1751–56
Joseph Hampton, (deceased,)	1757–67
Joseph Woolston, (*vice* Hampton, deceased,)	1767–76

Treasurers.

William Biles, (Deputy Treasurer,)	1684
William Biles,	1704
Jeremiah Langhorne,	1724–32
Thomas Janney,	1757
Abraham Chapman,	1761–67
Paul Preston,	1768–71
Joseph Chapman,	1772–76

Justices of the Peace.

James Harrison,	April	6, 1685
Thomas Janney,	April	6, 1685
William Yardley,	April	6, 1685
William Biles,	April	6, 1685
William Beaks,	April	6, 1685
John Otter,	April	6, 1685
Edmund Bennett,	April	6, 1685
John Swift,	April	6, 1685
Arthur Cook,	Jan.	2, 1689
Joseph Growden,	Jan.	2, 1689
William Yardley,	Jan.	2, 1689
Thomas Janney,	Jan.	2, 1689
William Biles,	Jan.	2, 1689
Nicholas Newlin,	Jan.	2, 1689
John Brock,	Jan.	2, 1689
Henry Baker,	Jan.	2, 1689
Gilbert Wheeler,	July	13, 1693
Joseph Wood,	July	13, 1693
John Brock,	July	15, 1693
Joseph Growden,	March	6, 1708
Joseph Kirkbride,	March	6, 1708
Willoughby Warder,	March	6, 1708
Edward Mayes,	March	6, 1708
Abel Janney,	March	6, 1708
Jeremiah Langhorne,	March	6, 1708
Thomas Stevenson,	March	6, 1708
Jonathan Scaife,	March	6, 1708
Samuel Baker,	March	6, 1708
Joseph Kirkbride,	Aug.	6, 1709
Thomas Stevenson,	Aug.	6, 1709
Joseph Growden,	March	3, 1710
Joseph Kirkbride,	March	3, 1710

Abel Janney,	March	3, 1710
Samuel Baker,	March	3, 1710
Francis White,	March	3, 1710
Jeremiah Langhorne,	March	3, 1710
Thomas Stevenson,	March	3, 1710
Thomas Watson,	March	3, 1710
John Rowland,	March	3, 1710
Willoughby Warder,	March	3, 1710
Jeremiah Langhorne,	May	1, 1712
Jeremiah Langhorne,	May	13, 1715
Joseph Kirkbride,	May	13, 1715
Thomas Stevenson,	May	13, 1715
Jeremiah Langhorne,	Dec.	30, 1715
Thomas Stevenson,	Dec.	30, 1715
Willoughby Warder,	Dec.	30, 1715
Anthony Burton,	Dec.	30, 1715
John Snowden,	Dec.	30, 1715
Francis White,	Dec.	30, 1715
Leonard Vandergrifts,	Dec.	30, 1715
Joseph Kirkbride,	Dec.	30, 1715
Thomas Watson,	Dec.	30, 1715
Everard Bolton,	Dec.	30, 1715
Thomas Watson, (Buckingham,)	Dec.	30, 1715
John Rowland,	Dec.	30, 1715
Christopher Vansandt,	Dec.	30, 1715
Joseph Kirkbride,	Sept.	6, 1718
Thomas Stevenson,	Sept.	6, 1718
Everard Bolton,	Sept.	6, 1718
William Biles,	Sept.	6, 1718
John Snowden,	Sept.	6, 1718
John Hall,	Sept.	6, 1718
Andrew Hamilton,	Sept.	6, 1718
Jeremiah Langhorne,	Sept.	6, 1718
Phineas Watson,	Sept.	6, 1718
Thomas Watson, (Buckingham,)	Sept.	6, 1718
Anthony Burton,	Sept.	6, 1718
Joseph Bond,	Sept.	6, 1718
Christopher Vansandt,	Sept.	6, 1718
Thomas Canby,	Dec.	12, 1719
Joseph Kirkbride,	Jan.	4, 1722
Thomas Watson,	Jan.	4, 1722
Anthony Burton,	Jan.	4, 1722
John Hall,	Jan.	4, 1722
Thomas Canby,	Jan.	4, 1722
Jeremiah Langhorne,	Jan.	4, 1722
William Biles,	Jan.	4, 1722

Joseph Bond, ...	Jan.	4, 1722
Christopher Vansandt, ...	Jan.	4, 1722

The above, with the exception of Thomas Watson
and Thomas Canby, re-commissioned with Joseph
Pidgeon, Joseph Kirkbride, Jr., Ambrose Barcroft,

and William Paxson, ...	Feb.	18, 1723
Joseph Kirkbride, ...	May	12, 1725
Jeremiah Langhorne, ...	May	12, 1725
William Biles, ...	May	12, 1725
Anthony Burton, ...	May	12, 1725
Joseph Bond, ...	May	12, 1725
Thomas Watson, ...	May	12, 1725
John Hall, ...	May	12, 1725
Christopher Vansandt, ...	May	12, 1725
Joseph Pidgeon, ...	May	12, 1725
Joseph Kirkbride, Jr., ...	May	12, 1725
Thomas Yardley, ...	May	12, 1725
William Paxson, ...	May	12, 1725
Thomas Canby, ...	May	12, 1725
Joseph Fell, ...	May	12, 1725

The above re-commissioned, except Joseph Bond,
with the addition of John Hart and Isaac Penning-

ton, ...	Sept.	14, 1725
Joseph Kirkbride, ...	Sept.	13, 1726
Jeremiah Langhorne, ...	Sept.	13, 1726
William Biles, ...	Sept.	13, 1726
Anthony Burton, ...	Sept.	13, 1726
Thomas Watson, (Strawberry bor.,) . . .	Sept.	13, 1726
John Hall.	Sept.	13, 1726
Christopher Vansandt, ...	Sept.	13, 1726
Joseph Pidgeon, ...	Sept.	13, 1726
Joseph Kirkbride, Jr., ...	Sept.	13, 1726
Thomas Yardley, ...	Sept.	13, 1726
William Paxson, ...	Sept.	13, 1726
Thomas Canby, ...	Sept.	13, 1726
Mathew Hughes, ...	Sept.	13, 1726
Benjamin Jones, ...	Sept.	13, 1726
Isaac Pennington, ...	Sept.	13, 1726
Thomas Watson, ...	May	13, 1715
Willoughby Warder, ...	May	13, 1715
Everard Bolton, ...	May	13, 1715
Anthony Burton, ...	May	13, 1715
Thomas Watson, (Buckingham,) . . .	May	13, 1715
John Snowden, ...	May	13, 1715
Joseph Kirkbride, ...	Sept.	10, 1717
Jeremiah Langhorn, ...	Sept.	10, 1717

Thomas Stevenson, ...	Sept.	10, 1717
Thomas Watson, ...	Sept.	10, 1717
Everard Bolton, ...	Sept.	10, 1717
Thomas Watson, (Buckingham,)	Sept.	10, 1717
William Biles, ...	Sept.	10, 1717
Anthony Burton, ...	Sept.	10, 1717
John Snowden, ...	Sept.	10, 1717
Joseph Bond, ...	Sept.	10, 1717
John Hall, ...	Sept.	10, 1717
Christopher Vansandt, ...	Sept.	10, 1717
Justices of the Peace now acting re-commissioned,	Dec.	1, 1733
John Wells, added, ...	Dec.	1, 1738
William Biles, ...	Nov.	22, 1738
Joseph Kirkbride, ...	Nov.	22, 1738
Thomas Canby, ...	Nov.	22, 1738
Thomas Yardley, ...	Nov.	22, 1738
Matthew Hughes, ...	Nov.	22, 1738
Lawrence Growden, ...	Nov.	22, 1738
Benjamin Jones, ...	Nov.	22, 1738
Isaac Pennington, ...	Nov.	22, 1738
Abraham Chapman, ...	Nov.	22, 1738
Simon Butler, ...	Nov.	22, 1738
John Wells, ...	Nov.	22, 1738
Eunion Williams, ...	Nov.	22, 1738
Anthony Burton, ...	Sept.	12, 1727
Thomas Watson, (Strawberry bor,) . . .	Sept.	12, 1727
John Hall, ...	Sept.	12, 1727
Christopher Vansandt, ...	Sept.	12, 1727
Joseph Pidgeon, ...	Sept.	12, 1727
Joseph Kirkbride, Jr., ...	Sept.	12, 1727
Thomas Yardley, ...	Sept.	12, 1727
William Paxson, ...	Sept.	12, 1727
Thomas Canby, ...	Sept.	12, 1727
Matthew Hughes, ...	Sept.	12, 1727
Benjamin Jones, ...	Sept.	12, 1727
Isaac Pennington, ...	Sept.	12, 1727
Matthew Rue, ...	Nov.	22, 1738
Richard Mitchell, of Durham, ...	Nov.	22, 1738
The Chief Burgess of Bristol, ...	Nov.	22, 1738
Joseph Kirkbride, ...	April	4, 1741
Matthew Hughes, ...	April	4, 1741
Lawrence Growden, ...	April	4, 1741
Benjamin Jones, ...	April	4, 1741
Isaac Pennington, ...	April	4, 1741
Simon Butler, ...	April	4, 1741
John Wells, ...	April	4, 1741

Ennion Williams,	April	4, 1741
Nathaniel Irish,	April	4, 1741
Matthew Rue,	April	4, 1741
Richard Mitchell,	April	4, 1741
Mark Watson,	April	4, 1741
Richard Hough,	April	4, 1741
Matthew Harvey,	April	4, 1741
The Chief Burgess of Bristol,	April	4, 1741
Joseph Kirkbride,	Dec.	17, 1745
Abraham Chapman,	Dec.	17, 1745
Matthew Hughes,	Dec.	17, 1745
Benjamin Jones,	Dec.	17, 1745
Simon Butler,	Dec.	17, 1745
John Wells,	Dec.	17, 1745
Ennion Williams,	Dec.	17, 1745
Matthew Rue,	Dec.	17, 1745
Richard Mitchell,	Dec.	17, 1745
Mark Watson,	Dec.	17, 1745
Richard Hough,	Dec.	17, 1745
John Abraham de Normandie,	Dec.	17, 1745
Robert Ellis,	Dec.	17, 1745
Alexander Brown Houston,	Dec.	17, 1745
John Jamison,	Dec.	17, 1745
Henry Antes,	Dec.	17, 1745
Thomas Owen,	Dec.	17, 1745
Thomas Craig,	Dec.	17, 1745
The Chief Burgess of Bristol for the time being,	Dec.	17, 1745
Lawrence Growden, (in separate commission,)	Dec.	17, 1745
Daniel Brodhead,	Sept.	25, 1747
Moses Depui,	Sept.	25, 1747
Abraham Chapman,	June	30, 1749
Matthew Hughes,	June	30, 1749
Simon Butler,	June	30, 1749
Ennion Williams,	June	30, 1749
Richard Mitchell,	June	30, 1749
Mark Watson,	June	30, 1749
John Abraham de Normandie,	June	30, 1749
Robert Ellis,	June	30, 1749
Alexander Graydon,	June	30, 1749
Henry Antes,	June	30, 1749
Thomas Owen,	June	30, 1749
Thomas Craig,	June	30, 1749
Daniel Brodhead,	June	30, 1749
Mahlon Kirkbride,	June	30, 1749
Langhorn Biles,	June	30, 1749
Thomas Janney,	June	30, 1749

Benjamin Griffith, ...	June	30, 1749
Richard Walker, ...	June	30, 1749
The Chief Burgess of Bristol for the time being,	June	30, 1749
Abraham Chapman, ...	June	9, 1752
Matthew Hughes, ...	June	9, 1752
Simon Butler, ...	June	9, 1752
Ennion Williams, ...	June	9, 1752
Richard Mitchell, ...	June	9, 1752
John Abraham de Normandie, ...	June	9, 1752
Alexander Graydon, ...	June	9, 1752
Mahlon Kirkbride, ...	June	9, 1752
Langhorne Biles, ...	June	9, 1752
Thomas Janney, ...	June	9, 1752
Richard Walker, ...	June	9, 1752
John Jamison, ...	June	9, 1752
William Buckley, ...	June	9, 1752
Septimus Robinson, ...	June	9, 1752
John Hart, ...	June	9, 1752
John Chapman, ...	June	9, 1752
John Wilson, ...	June	9, 1752
John Watson, Jr., ...	June	9, 1752
William Paxson, ...	June	9, 1752
William Rodman, ...	June	9, 1752
Gilbert Hicks, ...	June	9, 1752
The Chief Burgess of Bristol for the time being,	June	9, 1752
Alexander Graydon, ...	Feb.	28, 1761
Gilbert Hicks, ...	Feb.	28, 1761
Joseph Rockbuder, ...	Feb.	28, 1761
Thomas Janney, ...	Feb.	28, 1761
Joseph Hart, ...	Feb.	28, 1761
Richard Walker, ...	Feb.	28, 1761
Thomas Yardley, ...	Feb.	28, 1761
John Jamison, ...	Feb.	28, 1761
John Chapman, ...	Feb.	28, 1761
John Abraham de Normandie, . . .	Feb.	28, 1761
Jonathan Ingham, ...	Feb.	28, 1761
Jacob Bogart, ...	Feb.	28, 1761
George Taylor, ...	Feb.	28, 1761
William Folwell, ...	Feb.	28, 1761
Patrick Davis, ...	Feb.	28, 1761
The members of Council, ...	Dec.	7, 1764
Gilbert Hicks, ...	Dec.	7, 1764
Joseph Hart, ...	Dec.	7, 1764
Richard Walker, ...	Dec.	7, 1764
John Jamison, ...	Dec.	7, 1764
Jno. Abr. de Normandie, ...	Dec.	7, 1764

Jacob Bogart, ...	Dec.	7, 1764
Thomas Barnsley, ...	Dec.	7, 1764
Joseph Kirkbride, ...	Dec.	7, 1764
John Wilkinson, ...	Dec.	7, 1764
William Yardley, ...	Dec.	7, 1764
Henry Wynkoop, ...	Dec.	7, 1764
Robert Patterson, ...	Dec.	7, 1764
William Irwin, ...	Dec.	7, 1764
Benjamin Mathews, ...	Dec.	7, 1764
John Grier, ...	Dec.	7, 1764
John Harris, ...	Dec.	7, 1764
John Kidd, ...	May	14, 1767
John Kidd, ...	Oct.	1, 1767
Adam Hoops, ...	May	16, 1769
William Hicks,(*vice* Lawrence Growden, deceased,)	May	5, 1770
Members of Council, ...	May	23, 1770
Gilbert Hicks, ...	May	23, 1770
Joseph Hart, ...	May	23, 1770
Richard Walker, ...	May	23, 1770
John Jamison, ...	May	23, 1770
John Abraham de Normandie, ...	May	23, 1770
Jacob Bogart, ...	May	23, 1770
Thomas Barnsley, ...	May	23, 1770
Joseph Kirkbride, ...	May'	23, 1770
John Wilkinson, ...	May	23, 1770
William Yardley, ...	May	23, 1770
Henry Wynkoop, ...	May	23, 1770
Robert Patterson, ...	May	23, 1770
Benjamin Mathews, ...	May	23, 1770
John Harris, ...	May	23, 1770
Jonathan Ingham, ...	May	23, 1770
Hugh Hartshorne, ...	May	23, 1770
John Kidd, ...	May	23, 1770
Adam Hoopes, ...	May	23, 1770
William Hicks, ...	May	23, 1770
William Coxe, ...	May	23, 1770
Thomas Riché, ...	May	23, 1770
Turbutt Francis, (special commission,) . .	June	29, 1770
John Swift, (special commission,)	July	10, 1773
Gilbert Hicks, (Dedimus Potestatem,) . .	April	9, 1774
Joseph Hart, ...	April	9, 1774
Richard Walker, ...	April	9, 1774
John Jamison, ...	April	9, 1774
John Abraham de Normandie, (Dedimus Potestatem,)	April	9, 1774
Jacob Bogart, ...	April	9, 1774

Joseph Kirkbride, ...	April 9, 1774
John Wilkinson, ...	April 9, 1774
Henry Wynkoop, ...	April 9, 1774
Robert Patterson, ...	April 9, 1774
Benjamin Matthews, ...	April 9, 1774
Jonathan Ingham, ...	April 9, 1774
Hugh Hartshorne, ...	April 9. 1774
John Kidd, ...	April 9, 1774
William Coxe, ...	April 9, 1774
Thomas Riché, ...	April 9, 1774
Isaac Hicks, (Dedimus Potestatem,) . .	April 9, 1774
John Swift, ...	April 9, 1774
Thomas Foulke, ...	April 9, 1774
Francis Murray, ...	April 9, 1774
John Clarke, ...	August 8, 1775

Chief Burgesses of Bristol.

Joseph Bond, ...	Nov. 18, 1720
John Hall, ...	Sept. 12, 1721–27
John Abraham de Normandie, ...	Sept. 24, 1728–31
John Hall, ...	April 30, 1733
Ennion Williams, ...	Oct. 3, 1733–37
John Hall, ...	Oct. 17, 1738–41
John Abraham de Normandie, ...	Sept. 13, 1742–44
John Hall, ...	Sept. 11, 1745–46
William Buckley, ...	Sept. 12, 1747–54
Alexander Graydon, ...	Sept. 14, 1756
Hugh Hartshorne, ...	Sept. 19, 1760
John Hall, ...	Oct. 8, 1761
Hugh Hartshorne, ...	Sept. 15, 1762–63
John Priestley, ...	Sept. 17, 1764
Phineas Buckley, ...	Sept. 24, 1765–75

Second Burgess of Bristol.

Matthias Keen, ...	Sept. 12, 1747

High Constable of Bristol.

John Priestley, ...	Sept. 12, 1747

Assembly.

William Yardley, ...	1682–83
Samuel Darke, ...	1682–83
Robert Lucas, ...	1682–83
Nicholas Waln, ...	1682–83
John Wood, ...	1682–83
John Clowes, ...	1682–83

Thomas Fitzwater,	1682–83
Robert Hall,	1682–83
James Boyden,	1682–83
William Beaks,	1684
John Clowes,	1684
Richard Hough,	1684
John Otter,	1684
Edmond Bennett,	1684
William Beaks,	1685
Gilbert Wheeler,	1685
Henry Baker,	1685
William Darke,	1685
James Dilworth,	1685
Henry Paxson,	1685
William Yardley,	1686
Joseph Growden,	1686
John Otter,	1686
William Biles,	1686
Joshua Hoopes,	1686
John Rowland,	1686
Thomas Langhorne,	1687
Robert Hall,	1687
Nicholas Waln,	1687
Robert Lucas,	1687
Henry Baker,	1687
Edward Bennett,	1687
Nicholas Waln,	1688
Henry Baker,	1688
Richard Hough,	1688
Robert Lucas, (deceased,)	1688
Robert Hall, (deceased,)	1688
Joshua Hoopes,	1688
Arthur Cook, (Speaker,)	1689
William Biles,	1689
Phineas Pemberton,	1689
John Swift,	1689
Nicholas Waln,	1689
Edmund Bennett,	1689
Joseph Growdon, (Speaker,)	1690
Henry Painter,	1690
Richard Hough,	1690
Henry Baker,	1690
Edmund Bennett,	1690
John Cook,	1690
John Swift,	1692
John Otter,	1692

Joshua Hoopes, ... 1692
William Paxson, ... 1692
Nicholas Waln, ... 1692
John Rowland, ... 1692
Joseph Growden, (Speaker,) 1693
John Swift, ... 1693
Henry Painter, ... 1693
William Biles, ... 1694
Phineas Pemberton, ... 1694
Jonathan Scaife, ... 1694
Joshua Hoopes, ... 1695
Henry Paxson, ... 1695
Samuel Darke, ... 1695
Nicholas Waln, ... 1695
John Swift, ... 1695
Joseph Miller, ... 1695
William Biles, ... 1696
Joshua Hoopes, ... 1696
William Paxson, ... 1696
Joshua Hoopes, ... 1697
Stephen Beaks, ... 1697
Richard Hough, ... 1697
Jeremiah Langhorne, ... 1697
Phineas Pemberton, (Speaker,) 1698
Robert Heaton, ... 1698
Joseph Kirkbride, ... 1698
Henry Baker, ... 1698
John Surruff, ... 1699
John Swift, ... 1699
Richard Hough, ... 1699
Enoch Yardley, ... 1699
John Swift, ... 1700
Phineas Pemberton, ... 1700
Joshua Hoopes, ... 1700
William Paxson, ... 1700
Jeremiah Langhorne, ... 1700
Samuel Darke, ... 1700
Joseph Growden, (Speaker, extra session,) 1700
Richard Hough, (extra session,) 1700
Samuel Darke, (extra session,) 1700
Robert Heaton, (extra session,) 1700
Joseph Growden, (Speaker,) 1701
John Swift, ... 1701
Joshua Hoopes, ... 1701
William Paxson, ... 1701
William Biles, ... 1704

Joseph Growden, ... 1704
John Swift, ... 1704
Richard Hough, ... 1704
Jeremiah Langhorne, ... 1704
Henry Paxson, ... 1704
Thomas Watson, ... 1704
Peter Worrall, ... 1704
Joshua Hoopes, (*vice* Richard Hough, deceased,) . . 1705
Samuel Beaks, (*vice* Peter Worrall, deceased,) . . . 1705
Joseph Growden, (Speaker,) 1705
John Swift, ... 1705
Jeremiah Langhorne, ... 1705
Joshua Hoopes, ... 1705
Tobias Dymocke, ... 1705
Henry Paxson, ... 1705
Samuel Carpenter, ... 1705
William Paxson, ... 1705
John Swift, ... 1706
William Paxson, ... 1706
Joshua Hoopes, ... 1706
Henry Paxson, ... 1706
Samuel Darke, ... 1706
Thomas Hilborn, ... 1706
Ezra Croasdale, ... 1706
Thomas Harding, ... 1706
Henry Paxson, ... 1707
Samuel Darke, ... 1707
John Swift, ... 1707
William Paxson, ... 1707
Thomas Hilborn, ... 1707
William Biles, ... 1707
Ezra Croasdale, ... 1707
Samuel Beaks, ... 1707
William Paxson, ... 1708
William Biles, ... 1708
Joshua Hoopes, ... 1708
Henry Paxson, ... 1708
Samuel Darke, ... 1708
Samuel Beaks, ... 1708
Ezra Croasdale, ... 1708
Thomas Hilborn, ... 1708
Joshua Hoopes, ... 1709
Samuel Beaks, ... 1709
Samuel Darke, ... 1709
Ezra Croasdale, ... 1709
Robert Heaton, Jr., ... 1709

Henry Paxson,	1709
Thomas Hilborn,	1709
Thomas Harding,	1709
Abel Janney,	1710
John Clarke,	1710
Stoffel Vansant,	1710
John Hough,	1710
Thomas Stevenson,	1710
Samuel Baker,	1710
Jeremiah Langhorne,	1710
William Biles,	1710
Jeremiah Langhore,	1711
Thomas Stevenson,	1711
William Biles,	1711
Samuel Burgess, Jr.,	1711
Thomas Stackhouse,	1711
Joshua Hoopes,	1711
Robert Heaton, Jr.,	1711
Samuel Baker,	1711
Joseph Kirkbride,	1712
John Sotcher,	1712
Thomas Watson,	1712
Thomas Stevenson,	1712
Samuel Burges, (sick,)	1712
Stoffel Vansant,	1712
John Snowden,	1712
John Frost,	1712
John Swift, (vice Burges sick,)	1712
John Swift,	1713
Jeremiah Langhorne,	1713
Thomas Stevenson,	1713
William Stockdill,	1713
Thomas Watson, Jr.,	1713
Joseph Growden, (Speaker,)	1713
Thomas Stackhouse,	1713
Joseph Kirkbride,	1713
Joseph Kirkbride,	1714
Thomas Stevenson,	1714
Stoffel Vansant,	1714
Everard Bolton,	1714
Robert Harvey,	1714
John Swift,	1714
William Stockdill,	1714
William Paxson,	1714
Joseph Growden, (Speaker,)	1715
John Swift,	1715

157

John Sotcher,	1715
Thomas Yardley,	1715
Jeremiah Langhorne,	1715
Thomas Stackhouse,	1715
John Frost,	1715
Thomas Harding,	1715
Jeremiah Langhorne,	1716
Thomas Stevenson,	1716
John Sotcher,	1716
Joseph Bond,	1716
Joseph Kirkbride,	1716
Thomas Stackhouse, (refused to serve,)	1716
John Swift,	1716
James Carter, (refused to serve,)	1716
Samuel Beaks, *vice* Stackhouse,	1716–17
John Hall, *vice* Carter,	1716–17
Thomas Stevenson,	1717
Jeremiah Langhorne,	1717
John Sotcher,	1717
William Stockdill,	1717
William Paxson,	1717
Joseph Bond,	1717
Thomas Watson,	1717
Joseph Growden,	1717
William Biles,	1718
Thomas Stevenson,	1718
Jeremiah Langhorne,	1718
John Sotcher,	1718
Joseph Bond,	1718
William Paxson,	1718
Joseph Kirkbride,	1718
John Swift,	1718
Jeremiah Langhorne,	1719
John Sotcher,	1719
William Biles,	1719
Thomas Watson,	1719
Joseph Bond,	1719
William Paxson,	1719
Stoffell Vansant,	1719
William Stockdill,	1719
Jeremiah Langhorne,	1720
John Sotcher,	1720
William Biles,	1720
Thomas Watson,	1720
Joseph Bond,	1720
Henry Nelson,	1720

William Paxson,	1720
Joseph Kirkbride,	1720
Jeremiah Langhorne, (Speaker,)	1721
William Biles,	1721
John Sotcher,	1721
Joseph Fell,	1721
Abel Janney,	1721
Joseph Kirkbride, Jr.,	1721
Bartholomew Jacobs,	1721
Thomas Canby,	1721
Joseph Growden, (Speaker,)	1722
William Paxson,	1722
William Biles,	1722
John Sotcher,	1722
Joseph Kirkbride, Jr.,	1722
George Clough,	1722
Thomas Canby,	1722
Thomas Yardley,	1722
Jeremiah Langhorne,	1723
William Biles,	1723
Thomas Watson,	1723
Matthew Hughes,	1723
Joseph Fell,	1723
Christian Vanhorn,	1723
Abraham Chapman,	1723
Benjamin Jones,	1723
William Biles, (Speaker,)	1724
Jeremiah Langhorne,	1724
Joseph Fell,	1724
Christian Vanhorn,	1724
Matthew Hughes,	1724
Thomas Watson,	1724
Benjamin Jones,	1724
Abraham Chapman,	1724
Jeremiah Langhorne,	1725
William Biles,	1725
Joseph Fell,	1725
Abraham Chapman,	1725
Christian Vanhorn,	1725
Matthew Hughes,	1725
Benjamin Jones,	1725
Thomas Watson,	1725
Jeremiah Langhorne,	1726
Joseph Kirkbride,	1726
Abraham Chapman,	1726
Christian Vanhorn,	1726

159

Matthew Hughes,	1726
Richard Mitchell,	1726
Benjamin Jones,	1726
William Paxson,	1726
Joseph Kirkbride,	1727
Jeremiah Langhorne,	1727
William Paxson,	1727
Christian Vanhorn,	1727
Andrew Hamilton,	1727
Abraham Chapman,	1727
Benjamin Jones,	1727
Matthew Hughes,	1727
Joseph Kirkbride,	1728
Jeremiah Langhorne,	1728
William Paxson,	1728
Christian Vanhorn,	1728
Abraham Chapman,	1728
Matthew Hughes,	1728
Andrew Hamilton,	1728
Benjamin Jones,	1728
Joseph Kirkbride, Jr.,	1729
Jeremiah Langhorne,	1729
William Paxson,	1729
Abraham Chapman,	1729
Christian Vanhorn,	1729
Matthew Hughes,	1729
Benjamin Jones,	1729
Andrew Hamilton, (Speaker,)	1729
Joseph Kirkbride,	1730
William Paxson,	1730
Jeremiah Langhorne,	1730
Abraham Chapman,	1730
Christian Vanhorn,	1730
Andrew Hamilton, (Speaker,)	1730
Matthew Hughes,	1730
Thomas Canby,	1730
Joseph Kirkbride, Jr.,	1731
Jeremiah Langhorne,	1731
William Paxson,	1731
Christian Vanhorn,	1731
Abraham Chapman,	1731
Andrew Hamilton, (Speaker,)	1731
Matthew Hughes,	1731
Benjamin Jones,	1731
Joseph Kirkbride, Jr.,	1732
Jeremiah Langhorne,	1732

William Paxson,	1732
Abraham Chapman,	1732
Christian Vanhorn,	1732
Andrew Hamilton, (Speaker,)	1732
William Biles,	1732
Matthew Hughes,	1732
Joseph Kirkbride, Jr.,	1733
Abraham Chapman,	1733
Jeremiah Langhorn, (Speaker,)	1733
William Paxson, (deceased,)	1733
John Watson,	1733
Joseph Fell,	1733
Thomas Marriott,	1733
Thomas Canby,	1733
Andrew Hamilton, (*vice* Paxson, deceased,)	1733
Joseph Kirkbride, Jr.,	1734
Christian Vanhorn,	1734
Jeremiah Langhorne,	1734
Abraham Chapman,	1734
Andrew Hamilton, (Speaker,)	1734
William Biles,	1734
Thomas Marriott,	1734
Lawrence Growden,	1734
Joseph Kirkbride, Jr.,	1735
Christian Vanhorn,	1735
Jeremiah Langhorne,	1735
Andrew Hamilton, (Speaker,)	1735
William Biles,	1735
Lawrence Growden,	1735
Matthew Hughes,	1735
Benjamin Jones,	1735
Joseph Kirkbride, Jr.,	1736
Jeremiah Langhorne,	1736
Christian Vanhorn,	1736
Andrew Hamilton, (Speaker,)	1736
Lawrence Growden,	1736
William Biles,	1736
Matthew Hughes,	1736
Benjamin Jones,	1736
Jeremiah Langhorne,	1737
Joseph Kirkbride,	1737
Andrew Hamilton, (Speaker,)	1737
Lawrence Growden,	1737
Christian Vanhorn,	1737
William Biles,	1737
Benjamin Jones,	1737

161

Matthew Hughes,	1737
Jeremiah Langhorne,	1738
Joseph Kirkbride,	1738
Abraham Chapman,	1738
Andrew Hamilton,	1738
John Watson,	1738
Benjamin Field,	1738
Thomas Marriott,	1738
Thomas Canby,	1738
John Watson,	1739
Mark Watson,	1739
Thomas Canby, Jr.,	1739
Jeremiah Langhorne,	1739
Joseph Kirkbride,	1739
Abraham Chapman,	1739
Benjamin Field,	1739
Benjamin Jones,	1739
John Hall,	1740
Mark Watson,	1740
John Watson,	1740
Abraham Chapman,	1740
Benjamin Field,	1740
Thomas Canby, Jr.,	1740
Mahlon Kirkbride,	1740
Jeremiah Langhorne,	1740
John Hall,	1741
John Watson,	1741
Garret Vansant,	1741
Benjamin Field,	1741
Abraham Chapman,	1741
Mahlon Kirkbride,	1741
Joseph Shaw,	1741
Mark Watson,	1741
Mahlon Kirkbride,	1742
Mark Watson,	1742
John Watson,	1742
Abraham Chapman,	1742
John Hall,	1742
Benjamin Field,	1742
Joseph Shaw,	1742
Garret Vansant,	1742
Mahlon Kirkbride,	1743
John Watson,	1743
Abraham Chapman,	1743
John Hall,	1743
Mark Watson,	1743

Benjamin Field, ... 1743
Garret Vansant, ... 1743
Joseph Shaw, ... 1743
John Hall, ... 1744
Mark Watson, ... 1744
Mahlon Kirkbride, ... 1744
Abraham Chapman, ... 1744
Benjamin Field, ... 1744
John Watson, ... 1744
Garret Vansant, ... 1744
Joseph Shaw, ... 1744
John Hall, ... 1745
Mark Watson, ... 1745
Mahlon Kirkbride, ... 1745
Benjamin Field, ... 1745
Abraham Chapman, ... 1745
John Watson, ... 1745
Richard Mitchell, ... 1745
Cephas Child, ... 1745
Richard Mitchell, ... 1746
Derrick Hogeland, ... 1746
Abraham Chapman, ... 1746
Mahlon Kirkbride, ... 1746
John Watson, ... 1746
John Hall, ... 1746
Cephas Child, ... 1746
Joseph Hampton, ... 1746
Mahlon Kirkbride, ... 1747
Cephas Child, ... 1747
Joseph Hampton, ... 1747
Derrick Hogeland, ... 1747
Richard Walker, ... 1747
John Watson, ... 1747
Abraham Chapman, ... 1747
John Hall, ... 1747
Derrick Hogeland, ... 1748
Mahlon Kirkbride, ... 1748
Cephas Child, ... 1748
Joseph Hampton, ... 1748
Abraham Chapman, ... 1748
John Watson, ... 1748
George Logan, ... 1748
Richard Mitchell, ... 1748
John Woolston, ... 1749
Samuel Eastburn, ... 1749
Joseph Hampton, ... 1749

Mahlon Kirkbride, ...	1749
Richard Walker, ...	1749
Griffith Owen, ...	1749
Garret Vansant, ...	1749
John Hall, ...	1749
Mahlon Kirkbride, ...	1750
Joseph Hampton, ...	1750
John Woolston, ...	1750
Griffith Owen, ...	1750
John Hall, ...	1750
Garret Vansant, ...	1750
Richard Walker, ...	1750
Abraham Chapman, ...	1750
Mahlon Kirkbride, ...	1751
Joseph Hampton, ...	1751
Abraham Chapman, ...	1751
John Woolston, ...	1751
Griffith Owen, ...	1751
Richard Walker, ...	1751
Samuel Brown, ...	1751
Garret Vansant, ...	1751
Abraham Chapman, ...	1752
William Hoge, ...	1752
Joseph Hampton, ...	1752
Derrick Hogeland, ...	1752
Mahlon Kirkbride, ...	1752
Samuel Brown, ...	1752
Richard Walker, ...	1752
Griffith Owen, ...	1752
Mahlon Kirkbride, ...	1753
Joseph Hampton, ...	1753
Samuel Brown, ...	1753
William Hoge, ...	1753
Griffith Owen, ...	1753
Derrick Hogeland, ...	1753
Jonathan Ingham, ...	1753
William Smith, ...	1753
Mahlon Kirkbride, ...	1754
William Smith, ...	1754
Griffith Owen, ...	1754
Derrick Hogeland, ...	1754
Joseph Hampton, ...	1754
William Hoge, ...	1754
Jonathan Ingham, ...	1754
Samuel Brown, ...	1754
Mahlon Kirkbride, ...	1755

Joseph Hampton,	1755
Jonathan Ingham,	1755
Griffith Owen,	1755
Samuel Brown,	1755
Derrick Hogeland,	1755
William Smith,	1755
William Hoge,	1755
Griffith Owen,	1756
Richard Walker,	1756
Joseph Hampton,	1756
Mahlon Kirkbride, (resigned,)	1756
William Smith,	1756
James Melvin,	1756
William Hoge, (resigned,)	1756
Gabriel Vanhorn,	1756
John Abraham de Normandie, (*vice* Kirkbride, resigned,)	1756
Thomos Blackledge, (*vice* Hoge, resigned,)	1756
William Smith,	1757
John Abr. de Normandie, (deceased,)	1757
Griffith Owen,	1757
Gabriel Vanhorn,	1757
James Melvin,	1757
Thomas Blackledge,	1757
Richard Walker,	1757
Amos Strickland,	1757
Griffith Owen,	1758
William Smith,	1758
James Melvin,	1758
Amos Strickland,	1758
Benjamin Chapman,	1758
Joseph Watson,	1758
Derrick Hogeland,	1758
Joseph Kirkbride,	1758
Amos Strickland,	1759
Griffith Owen,	1759
Joseph Watson,	1759
Benjamin Chapman,	1759
James Melvin,	1759
William Smith,	1759
Jonathan Ingham,	1759
Jacob Bogart,	1759
Amos Strickland,	1760
James Melvin,	1760
Abraham Chapman,	1760
Joseph Hampton,	1760
Henry Wynkoop,	1760

165

Giles Knight,	1760
William Smith,	1760
George Ely,	1760
Giles Knight,	1761
James Melvin,	1761
Henry Wynkoop,	1761
Abraham Chapman,	1761
William Smith,	1761
John Wilkinson,	1761
Samuel Foulke,	1761
Samuel Browne,	1761
Samuel Foulke,	1762
Abraham Chapman,	1762
William Smith,	1762
James Melvin,	1762
John Wilkinson,	1762
Giles Knight,	1762
Samuel Browne,	1762
Henry Krewson,	1762
Samuel Foulke,	1763
Giles Knight,	1763
William Smith,	1763
Samuel Browne,	1763
Henry Krewson,	1763
Abraham Chapman,	1763
James Melvin,	1763
William Rodman,	1763
Giles Knight,	1764
William Rodman,	1764
Peter Shepherd,	1764
Samuel Foulke,	1764
Samuel Browne,	1764
William Smith,	1764
Henry Krewson,	1764
James Melvin,	1764
Giles Knight,	1765
Henry Krewson,	1765
Peter Shepherd,	1765
Samuel Foulke,	1765
William Rodman,	1765
James Melvin,	1765
William Smith,	1765
Samuel Browne,	1765
William Rodman,	1766
Samuel Foulke,	1766
Peter Shepherd,	1766

Samuel Browne, ... 1766
Henry Krewson, ... 1766
Benjamin Chapman, ... 1766
Joseph Hampton, ... 1766
James Melvin, ... 1766
Samuel Foulke, ... 1767
Peter Shepherd, ... 1767
Henry Krewson, ... 1767
Benjamin Chapman, ... 1767
William Rodman, ... 1767
Thomas Yardley, ... 1767
John Brown, ... 1767
Joseph Watson, ... 1767
William Rodman, ... 1768
Joseph Watson, ... 1768
Henry Krewson, ... 1768
John Brown, ... 1768
Peter Shepherd, ... 1768
Samuel Foulke, ... 1768
Benjamin Chapman, ... 1768
Giles Knight, ... 1768
Henry Krewson, ... 1769
John Brown, ... 1769
Peter Shepherd, ... 1769
Benjamin Chapman, ... 1769
Joseph Watson, ... 1769
Giles Knight, ... 1769
William Rodman, ... 1769
John Foulke, ... 1769
John Foulke, ... 1770
Peter Shepherd, ... 1770
John Brown, ... 1770
Henry Krewson, ... 1770
Joseph Watson, ... 1770
William Rodman, ... 1770
Benjamin Chapman, ... 1770
Joseph Galloway, (Speaker,) 1770
Joseph Galloway, (Speaker,) 1771
John Brown, ... 1771
William Rodman, ... 1771
John Foulke, ... 1771
Henry Krewson, ... 1771
Joseph Watson, ... 1771
Benjamin Chapman, ... 1771
Peter Shepherd, ... 1771
John Foulke, ... 1772

167

William Rodman,	1772
Henry Krewson,	1772
John Brown,	1772
Joseph Galloway, (Speaker,)	1772
Benjamin Chapman,	1772
Joseph Ellicott,	1772
Peter Shepherd,	1772
Joseph Ellicott,	1773
John Foulke,	1773
John Brown,	1773
Henry Krewson,	1773
Peter Shepherd,	1773
Joseph Galloway, (Speaker,)	1773
Benjamin Chapman,	1773
William Rodman,	1773
John Brown,	1774
John Foulke,	1774
William Rodman,	1774
Benjamin Chapman,	1774
Joseph Galloway,	1774
Robert Kirkbride,	1774
Gerardus Wynkoop,	1774
John Haney,	1774
William Rodman,	1775
John Haney,	1775
Gerardus Wynkoop,	1775
John Foulke,	1775
Benjamin Chapman,	1775
David Twining,	1775
John Brown,	1775
Thomas Jenks,	1775

PROVINCIAL OFFICERS

FOR THE

ADDITIONAL COUNTIES.

1729—1776.

OFFICERS FOR THE ADDITIONAL COUNTIES.

OFFICERS FOR LANCASTER COUNTY.

Sheriffs.

Robert Barber,	May 8, 1729,	Oct. 4, 1729
John Galbraith,		Oct. 3, 1730–31
Robert Buchanan,		Oct. 5, 1732–34
Samuel Smith,		Oct. 3, 1735–37
Robert Buchanan,		Oct. 4, 1738–40
James Mitchell,		Oct. 3, 1741
James Galbraith,		Oct. 4, 1742–43
John Sterrett,		Oct. 4, 1744
James Sterrett,		Oct. 5, 1745–47
Andrew Work,		Oct. 8, 1749–50
Robert Stewart,		Oct. 3, 1751
Thomas Smith,		Oct. 4, 1752–54
Joseph Pugh,		Oct. 5, 1755–57
William Smith,		Oct. 4, 1758–60
John Hay,		Oct. 5, 1761–63
John Barr,		Oct. 5, 1764–66
James Webb, Jr.,		Oct. 5, 1767–69
Frederick Stone,		Oct. 6, 1770–72
John Ferree,		Oct. 6, 1773–75

Coroners.

Andrew Galbraith,	May 8, 1729
Joshua Lowe,	Oct. 4, 1729–34
James Armstrong,	Oct. 3, 1735
Joshua Lowe,	Oct. 4, 1736
Michael McClure,	Oct. 4, 1737
Joshua Lowe,	Oct. 4, 1738–41
James Clark,	Oct. 4, 1742
John Morris,	Oct. 4, 1743
Robert Thompson,	Oct. 4, 1744
William Hamilton,	Oct. 5, 1745
Robert Wallace,	Oct. 4, 1746
Edward Dougherty,	Oct. 3, 1747–48

Robert Stewart, ... Oct. 8, 1749–50
Joseph Howard, ... Oct. 3, 1751
John Dougherty, ... Oct. 4, 1752–54
Matthias Slough, ... Oct. 4, 1755–68
Adam Reigart, ... Oct. 5, 1769
Samuel Boyd, ... Oct. 6, 1770–75

Barrack Masters.

James Webb, ... 1767–69
William Bausman, ... 1768–76

Sub-Sheriff.

Richard Loudon, ... 1738

Constable Paxtang Township.

James Alcorn, ... 1744

Justices for Trial of Negroes.

Emanuel Carpenter, ... Sept. 18, 1770
Isaac Saunders, ... Sept. 18, 1770
Emanuel Carpenter, ... Feb. 17, 1773
Isaac Saunders, ... Feb. 17, 1773

Justices of the Peace.

John Wright, ... May 8, 1729
Tobias Hendricks, ... May 8, 1729
Samuel Blunston, ... May 8, 1729
Andrew Cornish, ... May 8, 1729
Thomas Edwards, ... May 8, 1729
Caleb Peirce, ... May 8, 1729
Thomas Reid, ... May 8, 1729
Samuel Jones, ... May 8, 1729
Jeremiah Langhorne, ... April 18, 1732
All justices now acting, except Andrew Cornish,
  re-commissioned, ... Dec. 1, 1733
Edward Smout, ... Dec. 17, 1733
Derrick Updegrave, ... Dec. 17, 1733
Mark Evans, ... Aug. 24, 1736
John Wright, ... Jan. 25, 173$\frac{5}{6}$
Tobias Hendricks, ... Jan. 25, 173$\frac{5}{6}$
Samuel Blunston, ... Jan. 25, 173$\frac{5}{6}$
Thomas Edwards, ... Jan. 25, 173$\frac{5}{6}$
Samuel Jones, ... Jan. 25, 173$\frac{5}{6}$
Andrew Galbraith, ... Jan. 25, 173$\frac{5}{6}$
Edward Smout, ... Jan. 25, 173$\frac{5}{6}$
Derrick Updegrave, ... Jan. 25, 173$\frac{5}{7}$

172

Mark Evans,	Jan.	25, 173⅞
John Caldwell,	Jan.	25, 173⅞
James Whitehill,	Jan.	25, 173⅞
Emanuel Carpenter,	Jan.	25, 173⅞
John Wright,	Nov.	22, 1738
Tobias Hendricks,	Nov.	22, 1738
Samuel Blunston,	Nov.	22, 1738
Thomas Edwards,	Nov.	22, 1738
Samuel Jones,	Nov.	22, 1738
Andrew Galbraith,	Nov.	22, 1738
Edward Smout,	Nov.	22, 1738
Samuel Smith, of Conewago,	Nov.	22, 1738
Thomas Lindley,	Nov.	22, 1738
Emanuel Carpenter,	Nov.	22, 1738
Anthony Shaw,	Nov.	22, 1738
Thomas Cookson,	Nov.	22, 1738
John Coyle,	Nov.	22, 1738
John Kyle, of Chestnut Level,	Nov.	22, 1738
James Armstrong,	Nov.	22, 1738
Samuel Boyd,	Nov.	22, 1738
Thomas Edwards,	April	4, 1741
Samuel Jones,	April	4, 1741
Andrew Galbraith,	April	4, 1741
Edward Smout,	April	4, 1741
Samuel Smith, of Conewago,	April	4, 1741
Emanuel Carpenter,	April	4, 1741
Thomas Cookson,	April	4, 1741
John Kyle,	April	4, 1741
James Armstrong,	April	4, 1741
Samuel Smith, of Conewago,	April	4, 1741
Samuel Boyd,	April	4, 1741
Andrew Douglass,	April	4, 1741
Richard Ocaihan, (O'Kane,)	April	4, 1741
John Hogg,	April	4, 1741
Conrad Weiser,	April	4, 1741
John Reynolds	April	4, 1741
James Whitehill, of Salisbury,	April	4, 1741
James Lewis, of Tulpehocken,	April	4, 1741
David Jones, of Pequa,	April	4, 1741
Thomas Edwards,	Dec.	17, 1745
Andrew Galbraith,	Dec.	17, 1745
Edward Smout,	Dec.	17, 1745
Emanuel Carpenter,	Dec.	17, 1745
John Kyle,	Dec.	17, 1745
Conrad Weiser,	Dec.	17, 1745
James Armstrong,	Dec.	17, 1745

173

Samuel Smith, ...	Dec.	17, 1745
John Hogg, ...	Dec.	17, 1745
James Whitehill, ...	Dec.	17, 1745
David Jones, ...	Dec.	17, 1745
James Galbraith, ...	Dec.	17, 1745
John Postlethwaite, ...	Dec.	17, 1745
William Maxwell, ...	Dec.	17, 1745
James Gillaspy, ...	Dec.	17, 1745
Samuel Anderson, ...	Dec.	17, 1745
Edward Berwick, ...	Dec.	17, 1745
Henry Harris, Cumru Tp., ...	Dec.	17, 1745
The Chief Burgess of Lancaster, for the time being,	Dec.	17, 1745
Thomas Cookson, (separate commission,) .	Dec.	17, 1745
Thomas Edwards, ...	April	22, 1749
Edward Smout, ...	April	22, 1749
Emanuel Carpenter, ...	April	22, 1749
Conrad Weiser, ...	April	22, 1749
Samuel Smith, ...	April	22, 1749
John Kyle, ...	April	22, 1749
James Galbraith, ...	April	22, 1749
Thomas Cookson, ...	April	22, 1749
James Whitehill, ...	April	22, 1749
Edward Berwick, ...	April	22, 1749
James Gillaspy, ...	April	22, 1749
William Maxwell, ...	April	22, 1749
Samuel Anderson, ...	April	22, 1749
John Postlethwaite, ...	April	22, 1748
George Swope, ...	April	22, 1749
The Chief Burgess of Lancaster for time being,	April	22, 1749
William Parsons, ...	April	22, 1749
Bernard Van Leer, ...	April	22, 1749
James Wright, ...	April	22, 1749
James Webb, ...	April	22, 1749
George Croghan, ...	April	22, 1749
William Hartley, ...	April	22, 1749
Thomas Foster, ...	April	22, 1749
David McClure, ...	April	22, 1749
James Smith, ...	April	22, 1749
John Day, ...	April	22, 1749
Robert Dunning, ...	April	22, 1749
Robert Harris, ...	April	22, 1749
Patrick Watson, ...	April	22, 1749
Matthew Dill, ...	April	22, 1749
Jedediah Alexander, ...	April	22, 1749
William Parsons, ...	June	10, 1752
Thomas Edwards, ...	Oct.	16, 1752

Lynford Lardner, ...	Oct.	16, 1752
Emanuel Carpenter.	Oct.	16, 1752
James Galbraith, ...	Oct.	16, 1752
John Kyle, ...	Oct.	16, 1752
Thomas Cookson, ...	Oct.	16, 1752
James Whitehill, ...	Oct.	16, 1752
James Wright, ...	Oct.	16, 1752
Adam Simon Kuhn, ...	Oct.	16, 1752
James Smith, ...	Oct.	16, 1752
Samuel Anderson, ...	Oct.	16, 1752
Thomas Foster, ...	Oct.	16, 1752
John Allison, ...	Oct.	16, 1752
William Jevon, ...	Oct.	16, 1752
Robert Thompson, ...	Oct.	16, 1752
Thomas Holliday, ...	Oct.	16, 1752
Adam Read, ...	Oct.	16, 1752
Edward Shippen, ...	March	28, 1753
Emanuel Carpenter, ...	Jan.	30, 1761
Isaac Saunders, ...	Jan.	30, 1761
William Jevon, ...	Jan.	30, 1761
Adam Simon Kuhn, ...	Jan.	30, 1761
Robert Thompson, ...	Jan.	30, 1761
Edward Shippen, ...	Jan.	30, 1761
Andrew Work, ...	Jan.	30, 1761
John Allison, ...	Jan.	30, 1761
Calvin Cooper, ...	Jan.	30, 1761
Adam Read, ...	Jan.	30, 1761
Thomas Foster, ...	Jan.	30, 1761
Isaac Richardson, ...	Jan.	30, 1761
John Hay, ...	Jan.	30, 1761
Zaccheus Davis, ...	Jan.	30, 1761
William Hamilton, ...	Jan.	30, 1761
Emanuel Carpenter, ...	April	24, 1764
Isaac Saunders, ...	April	24, 1764
Edward Shippen, ...	April	24, 1764
William Jevon, ...	April	24, 1764
Adam Simon Kuhn, ...	April	24, 1764
Robert Thompson, ...	April	24, 1764
Andrew Work, ...	April	24, 1764
John Allison, ...	April	24, 1764
Calvin Cooper, ...	April	24, 1764
Adam Read, ...	April	24, 1764
Thomas Foster, ...	April	24, 1764
James Burd, ...	April	24, 1764
Isaac Richardson, ...	April	24, 1764
John Hay, ...	April	24, 1764

175

Zacheus Davis,	April	24, 1764
William Hamilton,	April	24, 1764
And Members of Council,	April	24, 1764
Robert Boyd, (of borough of Lancaster,)	June	20, 1769
Members of Council,	May	23, 1770
Emanuel Carpenter,	May	23, 1770
Isaac Saunders,	May	23, 1770
Edward Shippen,	May	23, 1770
Adam Simon Kuhn,	May	23, 1770
Calvin Cooper,	May	23, 1770
James Burd,	May	23, 1770
Zaccheus Davis,	May	23, 1770
John Philip DeHaas,	May	23, 1770
James Clemson,	May	23, 1770
James Bickham,	May	23, 1770
Robert Boyd,	May	23, 1770
Timothy Green,	May	23, 1770
James Work,	May	23, 1770
Everhart Gruber,	May	23, 1770
William Henry,	May	23, 1770

Treasurers.

Bernard Hubley,	1757–58–59
Mattthias Slough,	1762–69
Michael Diffenderfer,	1770–72
Christian Wirtz,	1773–76

Collectors.

James Mitchell,	1731–43
Arthur Patterson,	1744–56
James Webb,	1757–68
Sebastian Graf,	1770–76

Chief Burgesses of Lancaster.

John Dehuff,	Sept. 21, 1744
Peter Worrall,	Sept. 18, 1746–47–48
Adam Simon Kuhn,	Sept. —, 1749–53
Samuel Boude,	Sept. 22, 1761
James Bickham,	Sept. 24, 1762–63
William Bausman,	Sept. 22, 1762
William A. Atlee,	Sept. 23, 1773

Prothonotary, Register, and Recorder.

William Parsons,	May 6, 1752
Edward Shippen,	Mar. 28, 1753–75

LANCASTER COUNTY.

Clerk of Quarter Sessions.

Edward Shippen, ... April 20, 1753

Assembly.

Thomas Edwards,	1729
John Wright,	1729
James Mitchell,	1729
Thomas Read,	1729
John Wright,	1730
Thomas Edwards,	1730
George Stewart,	1730
John Musgrove,	1730
John Coyle,	1731
Andrew Galbraith,	1731
John Musgrove,	1731
Thomas Edwards,	1731
George Stewart,	1732
Thomas Edwards,	1732
Samuel Blunston,	1732
Andrew Galbraith,	1732
Andrew Galbraith,	1733
Thomas Edwards,	1733
John Wright,	1733
John Coyle,	1733
James Hamilton,	1734
John Emerson,	1734
Andrew Galbraith,	1734
John Wright,	1734
James Hamilton,	1735
Thomas Edwards,	1735
Andrew Galbraith,	1735
Thomas Amstrong,	1735
James Hamilton,	1736
Andrew Galbraith,	1736
Thomas Armstrong,	1736
Thomas Edwards,	1736
James Hamilton,	1737
Andrew Galbraith,	1737
John Wright,	1737
Samuel Smith,	1737
James Hamilton,	1738
Andrew Galbraith,	1738
Samuel Smith,	1738
John Wright,	1738
John Wright,	1739

177

Thomas Ewing, ...	1739
Thomas Lindley, ...	1739
Thomas Edwards, ...	1739
Thomas Lindley, ...	1740
John Wright, ...	1740
Thomas Ewing, ...	1740
Anthony Shaw, ...	1740
Thomas Lindley, ...	1741
John Wright, ...	1741
Samuel Blunston, ...	1741
Anthony Shaw, ...	1741
Samuel Blunston, ...	1742
John Wright, ...	1742
Thomas Lindley, ...	1742
Anthony Shaw, ...	1742
Anthony Shaw, ...	1743
Arthur Patterson, ...	1743
Thomas Lindley, deceased, ...	1743
John Wright, ...	1743
Samuel Blunston, (*vice* Lindley, deceased,)	1743
James Mitchell, ...	1744
John Wright, ...	1744
Arthur Patterson, ...	1744
Samuel Blunston, ...	1744
John Wright, (Speaker,)	1745
James Mitchell, ...	1745
Arthur Patterson, ...	1745
James Wright, ...	1745
John Wright, ...	1746
James Mitchell, ...	1746
Arthur Patterson, ...	1746
James Wright, ...	1746
John Wright, ...	1747
Arthur Patterson, ...	1747
James Webb, ...	1747
Peter Worrall, ...	1747
John Wright, ...	1748
Arthur Patterson, ...	1748
James Webb, ...	1748
Peter Worrall, ...	1748
Arthur Patterson, ...	1749
James Wright, ...	1749
Peter Worrall, ...	1749
Calvin Cooper, ...	1749
Arthur Patterson, ...	1750
Calvin Cooper, ...	1750

James Wright, ...	1750
James Webb, ...	1750
Arthur Patterson, ...	1751
Calvin Cooper, ...	1751
James Wright, ...	1751
Peter Worrall, ...	1751
Arthur Patterson, ...	1752
Calvin Cooper, ...	1752
Peter Worrall, ...	1752
James Wright, ...	1752
Arthur Patterson, ...	1753
James Wright, ...	1753
Calvin Cooper, ...	1753
Peter Worrall, ...	1753
James Wright, ...	1754
Calvin Cooper, ...	1754
Arthur Patterson, ...	1754
Peter Worrall, ...	1754
James Wright, ...	1755
James Webb, ...	1755
Calvin Cooper, ...	1755
Peter Worrall, ...	1755
Emanuel Carpenter, ...	1756
James Wright, ...	1756
James Webb, ...	1756
John Douglass, ...	1756
James Wright, ...	1757
James Webb, ...	1757
Emanuel Carpenter, ...	1757
Isaac Saunders, ...	1757
Emanuel Carpenter, ...	1758
Isaac Saunders, ...	1758
James Webb, ...	1758
James Wright, ...	1758
James Webb, ...	1759
Emanuel Carpenter, ...	1759
Isaac Saunders, ...	1759
James Wright, ...	1759
Emanuel Carpenter, ...	1760
Isaac Saunders, ...	1760
James Webb, ...	1760
James Wright, ...	1760
Emanuel Carpenter, ...	1761
James Wright, ...	1761
James Webb, ...	1761
John Douglass, ...	1761

John Douglass,	1762
James Webb,	1762
Emanuel Carpenter,	1762
James Wright,	1762
Emanuel Carpenter,	1763
James Wright,	1763
John Douglass,	1763
Isaac Saunders,	1763
Emanuel Carpenter,	1764
James Wright,	1764
Isaac Saunders,	1764
James Webb,	1764
Emanuel Carpenter,	1765
James Wright,	1765
James Webb,	1765
Jacob Carpenter,	1765
Emanuel Carpenter,	1766
James Wright,	1766
James Webb,	1766
Jacob Carpenter,	1766
Emanuel Carpenter,	1767
James Wright,	1767
Jacob Carpenter,	1767
James Webb,	1767
Emanuel Carpenter,	1768
James Webb,	1768
Jacob Carpenter,	1768
George Ross,	1768
Emanuel Carpenter,	1769
Jacob Carpenter,	1769
James Webb,	1769
George Ross,	1769
Emanuel Carpenter,	1770
George Ross,	1770
James Wright,	1770
Joseph Ferree,	1770
Emanuel Carpenter,	1771
George Ross,	1771
Joseph Ferree,	1771
William Downing,	1771
Joseph Ferree,	1772
Jacob Carpenter,	1772
Isaac Whitelock,	1772
James Webb,	1772
Joseph Ferree,	1773
James Webb,	1773

YORK COUNTY.

George Ross,	1773
Matthias Slough,	1773
James Webb,	1774
Joseph Ferree,	1774
Matthias Slough,	1774
George Ross,	1774
Curtis Grubb,	1775
Matthias Slough,	1775
George Ross,	1775
James Webb,	1775
Thomas Porter, (additional,)	1776
Bartrem Galbraith, (additional,)	1776

OFFICERS FOR YORK COUNTY.

Sheriffs.

Hance Hamilton,	Oct. 8, 1749–51
John Adlum,	Oct. 4, 1752–54
Joseph Adlum,	Oct. 4, 1755
Thomas Hamilton,	Oct. 5, 1756
John Adlum,	1758
Peter Shugart,	Oct. 4, 1759
Zachariah Shugart,	Oct. 3, 1760
Peter Shugart,	Oct. 5, 1761
Robert McPherson,	Oct. 4, 1762–64
David McConaughy,	Oct. 4, 1765–67
George Eichelberger,	Oct. 6, 1768–70
Samuel Edie,	Oct. 5, 1771–73
Charles Lukens,	Oct. 6, 1774–75

Coronors.

Nicholas Ryland,	Oct. 8, 1749
Alexander Love,	Oct. 3, 1751–53
Archibald McGrew,	Oct. 4, 1754
Zachariah Shugart,	Oct. 4, 1755–56
William King,	Oct. 4, 1759–60
Michael Swope,	Oct. 5, 1761–62
John Adlum,	Oct. 4, 1763–64
James Walker,	Oct. 4, 1765
Joseph Adlum,	Oct. 4, 1766
John Adlum,	Oct. 6, 1767
Joseph Adlum,	Oct. 6, 1768–75

Prothonotary, Register and Recorder, Clerk of Court.

George Stevenson,	Sept. 23, 1749–58
Samuel Johnston,	Oct. 4, 1764–74

Clerk of the Market.

Henry Longberger,	1774

Collectors of Excise.

David McConaughy,	1749–56
Thomas Minshall,	1757–66
George Eichelberger,	1767–69
Jacob Billmyer,	1770–72
Henry Miller,	1772–75
Michael Hahn,	1775–76

Treasurers.

David McConaughy, appointed,	Dec.	1749
Thomas McCartney,	Dec.	1752
Hugh Whitford,		1754
Robert MPherson,		1755
Frederick Galwick,	Nov.	1756
William Delap,		1757
John Blackburn,	Dec.	1759
David McConaughy,	Oct.	1764
John Blackburn, (deceased,)		1766
Robert McPherson,	Aug.	1767
Michael Swope,	Oct.	1769

Commissioners.

First Class.

George Schwabe,	qualified on Oct.	31, 1749
Bartholomew Maule,	Oct.	29, 1751
Peter Shugart,	Oct.	1754
Martin Eichelberger,	Oct.	1757
James Welsh,	Oct.	1760
William Douglass,	Oct.	1763
Joseph Updegraff,	Oct.	1766
John Heckendorn,	Oct.	31, 1769
John Hay,	Oct.	20, 1772
Michael Hahn,	Oct.	1775
William Ross,		1776–7

Second Class.

Walter Sharp,	qualified on Oct.	31, 1749
William McClellan,	Oct.	30, 1750

John Mickley, ...	Oct.	1752
Thomas McCartney, ...	Oct.	28, 1755
William Delap, ...	Oct.	1758
George Meyers, ...	Oct.	31, 1761
Philip Ziegler, ...	Oct.	1764
Hugh Dunwoodie, ...	Oct.	1767
John Monteith, ...	Oct.	15, 1770
Henry Tyson, ...	Oct.	20, 1773
John Hay, ...	Oct.	1776

Third Cla s.

Patrick Watson, ... qualified on	Oct.	31, 1749
James Agnew, ...	Oct.	30, 1753
Robert McPherson, ...	Oct.	1756
John Frankelberger, ...	Oct.	31, 1758
John Adlum, ...	Oct.	30, 1759
Samuel Edie, ...	Oct.	1762
Thomas Stockton, ...	Oct.	1765
William Gemmill, ...	Oct.	27, 1768

Justices of the Peace.

George Stevenson, ...	Sept.	23, 1749
Harman Updegrave, ...		1758
Members of Council, ...	Oct.	17, 1764
John Blackburn, ...	Oct.	17, 1764
David Jameson, ...	Oct.	17, 1764
Martin Eichelberger, ...	Oct.	17, 1764
Archibald McGrew, ...	Oct.	17, 1764
Samuel Johnston, ...	Oct.	17, 1764
Samuel Edie, ...	Oct.	17, 1764
Matthew Dill, ...	Oct.	17, 1764
Michael Swope, ...	Oct.	17, 1764
James Welsh, ...	Oct.	17, 1764
Robert McPherson, ...	Oct.	17, 1764
John Smith, ...	Oct.	17, 1764
Henry Schlegel, ...	Oct.	17, 1764
Thomas Minshall, ...	Oct.	17. 1764
Conyngham Sample, ...	Oct.	17, 1764
William Dunlap, ...	Oct.	17. 1764
Joseph Hutton, ...	Oct.	17, 1764
John Adlum, (special commission,) . . .	Dec.	7, 1764
William Smith, (special commission,) . . .	Dec.	7, 1764
John Pope, ...	July	23. 1768
Robert McPherson, ...	Mar.	11, 1771
David Jameson, ...	Mar.	11, 1771
Martin Eichelberger, ...	Mar.	11, 1771

Archibald McGrew,	March	11, 1771
John Adlum,	March	11, 1771
John Pope,	March	11, 1771
Michael Swope,	March	11, 1771
Samuel Johnston,	March	11, 1771
Samuel Edie,	March	11, 1771
William Delap,	March	11, 1771
Thomas Minshall,	March	11, 1771
Matthew Dill,	March	11, 1771
Henry Schlegle,	March	11, 1771
William Smith,	March	11, 1771
John Smith,	March	11, 1771
Conyngham Sample,	March	11, 1771
Richard McAllister,	March	11, 1771
David McConaughy,	March	11, 1771
William Penrose,	March	11, 1771
William Rankin,	March	11, 1771
Joseph Updegrave,	March	11, 1771
Robert McPherson, (Dedimus Potestatem,)	April	9, 1774
David Jameson,	April	9, 1774
Martin Eichelberger,	April	9, 1774
Archibald McGrew,	April	9, 1774
John Pope,	April	9, 1774
Samuel Johnston, (Dedimus Potestatem,)	April	9, 1774
Samuel Edie,	April	9, 1774
William Delap,	April	9, 1774
Matthew Dill,	April	9, 1774
Henry Schlegle,	April	9, 1774
William Smith,	April	9, 1774
John Smith,	April	9, 1774
Conyngham Sample,	April	9, 1774
Richard McAllister,	April	9, 1774
David McConaughy,	April	9, 1774
William Rankin,	April	9, 1774
Joseph Updegrave,	April	9, 1774
William Scott,	April	9, 1774
Joseph Donaldson,	April	9, 1774
William Leas,	April	9, 1774
William Bailey,	April	9, 1774
James Ewing,	Sept.	27, 1774
William McClean,	Sept.	27, 1774
Thomas Latta,	Sept.	27, 1774
William McCaskey,	Sept.	27, 1774
Josiah Scott,	Sept.	27, 1774

YORK COUNTY.

Justices for trial of Negroes.

David Jamison, ...	July	15, 1768
Martin Eichelberger, ...	July	15, 1768

Assembly.

John Wright, ...	1749
John Armstrong, ...	1749
John Wright, ...	1751
John Witherow, ...	1751
John Wright, ...	1752
David McConaughy, ...	1752
John Wright, ...	1753
David McConaughy, ...	1753
John Wright, ...	1754
David McConaughy, ...	1754
John Wright, ...	1755
David McConaughy, ...	1755
David McConaughy, ...	1756
John Wright, ...	1756
John Wright, ...	1757
David McConaughy, ...	1757
John Wright, ...	1758
David McConaughy, ...	1758
John Wright, ...	1759
David McConaughy, ...	1759
David McConaughy, ...	1760
John Blackburn, ...	1760
John Blackburn, ...	1761
David McConaughy, ...	1761
David McConaughy, ...	1762
John Blackburn, ...	1762
David McConaughy, ...	1763
John Blackburn, ...	1763
David McConaughy, ...	1764
John Blackburn, ...	1764
John Blackburn, ...	1765
Robert McPherson, ...	1765
John Blackburn, ...	1766
Robert McPherson, ...	1766
Robert McPherson, ...	1767
Archibald McGrew, ...	1767
Thomas Minshall, ...	1768
Michael Swope, ...	1768
Michael Swope, ...	1769
Thomas Minshall, ...	1769
Michael Swope, ...	1770

185

Thomas Minshall, ... 1770
Michael Swope, ... 1771
James Ewing, ... 1771
James Ewing, ... 1772
John Pope, ... 1772
James Ewing, ... 1773
John Pope, ... 1773
James Ewing, ... 1774
Michael Swope, ... 1774
James Ewing, ... 1775
Michael Swope, ... 1775
Samuel Edie, (additional,) 1776
James Rankin, (additional,) 1776

OFFICERS FOR BERKS COUNTY.

Sheriffs.

Benjamin Lightfoot, ... Oct. 4, 1752–54
William Boone, ... Oct. 4, 1755–56
Jacob Weaver, ... Oct. 4, 1759–60
Henry Christ, ... Oct. 5, 1761–62
Jacob Weaver, ... Oct. 4, 1763–64
Jasper Scull, ... Oct. 4, 1765–67
Jacob Shoemaker, ... Oct. 4, 1768–70
George Nagle, ... Oct. 5, 1771–73
Henry Vanderslice, ... Oct. 5, 1774–75

Coroners.

William Boone, ... Oct. 4, 1752–54
Benjamin Parvon, ... Oct. 4, 1755
John Warren, ... Oct. 4, 1759
Jacob Kern, ... Oct. 3, 1760–61
Adam Witman, ... Oct. 4, 1762
Samuel Weiser, ... Oct. 4, 1763–65
Christopher Witman, ... Oct. 4, 1766
Henry Haller, ... Oct. 5, 1767
James Whitehead, Jr., ... Oct. 4, 1768–69
Samuel Jackson, ... Oct. 4, 1770
Isaac Levan, Jr., ... Oct. 5, 1771–72
Peter Brecht, ... Oct. 4, 1773–75

Collectors.

John Hughes, (deceased,) 1752–63

BERKS COUNTY.

John Patton,	1764
Jasper Scull,	1765–73
John Biddle,	1773–6

Treasurers.

Jonas Seely,	1757–68
Christopher Witman,	1769–76

Prothonotary, Clerk Orphans' Court, Recorder, and Clerk of the Peace.

James Read,	June 4, 1752

Clerk of the Market.

Henry Haller,	1774

Judge of Oyer and Terminer.

Alexander Stedman,	Feb. 4, 1764

Justices of the Peace.

Francis Parvin,	Feb.	7, 1761
Jonas Seely,	Feb.	7, 1761
William Bird,	Feb.	7, 1761
William Maugridge,	Feb.	7, 1761
Jacob Levan,	Feb.	7, 1761
James Read,	Feb.	7, 1761
Peter Spyker,	Feb.	7, 1761
Joseph Millard,	Feb.	7, 1761
Benjamin Lightfoot,	Feb.	7, 1761
George Webb,	Feb.	7, 1761
Members of Council,	April	24, 1764
Jonas Seely,	April	24, 1764
Wiliam Maugridge, (deceased, 1766,)	April	24, 1764
Peter Spyker,	April	24, 1764
Jacob Levan, (deceased, 1766,)	April	24, 1764
James Read,	April	24, 1764
George Webb,	April	24, 1764
Joseph Millard,	April	24, 1764
Thomas Rutter,	April	24, 1764
Jacob Morgan,	April	24, 1764
James Deimer,	April	24, 1764
John Patton,	April	24, 1764
George Douglass,	April	24, 1764
Henry Christ,	April	24, 1764
Sebastian Zimmerman,	Nov.	7, 1766
Nicholas Harmony,	Nov.	7, 1766

Jonas Seely,	May,	1769
James Read,	May,	1769
Peter Spyker,	May,	1769
George Webb,	May,	1769
Joseph Millard,	May,	1769
Thomas Rutter,	May,	1769
Jacob Morgan,	May,	1769
James Deimer,	May,	1769
John Patton,	May,	1769
George Douglass,	May,	1769
Henry Christ,	May,	1769
Sebastian Zimmerman,	May,	1769
Nicholas Harmony,	May,	1769
John Potts,	May	8, 1752
Conrad Weiser,	May	8, 1752
Francis Parvin,	May	8, 1752
Anthony Lee,	May	8, 1752
Jonas Seely,	May	8, 1752
Henry Harvey,	May	8, 1752
William Bird,	May	8, 1752
William Maugridge,	May	8, 1752
Moses Starr,	May	8, 1752
James Boone,	May	8, 1752
Jacob Levan,	May	8, 1752
James Read,	May	8, 1752
Members of Council,	May	23, 1770
Benjamin Lightfoot,	May	23, 1770
James Read,	May	23, 1770
John Patton,	May	23, 1770
George Douglass,	May	23, 1770
Peter Spyker,	May	23, 1770
George Webb,	May	23, 1770
Thomas Rutter,	May	23, 1770
Jacob Morgan,	May	23, 1770
James Deimer,	May	23, 1770
Henry Christ,	May	23, 1770
Sebastian Zimmerman,	May	23, 1770
Mark Bird,	May	23, 1770
William Reeser,	May	23, 1773
Daniel Brodhead,	July	9, 1771
Jonathan Potts.		
Balthazer Gehr.		
Thomas Dunlap.		
Benjamin Lightfoot,		1773
James Read,		1773
Peter Spyker,		1773

George Webb, ... 1773
Thomas Rutter, ... 1773
Jacob Morgan, ... 1773
James Deimer, ... 1773
John Patton, ... 1773
George Douglass, ... 1773
Henry Christ, ... 1773
Sebastian Zimmerman, ... 1773
Mark Bird, ... 1773
William Reeser, ... 1773
Daniel Brodhead, ... 1773

Assembly.

Moses Starr, ... 1752
Moses Starr, ... 1753
Moses Starr, ... 1754
Francis Parvin, ... 1755
Thomas Yorke, ... 1756
Thomas Yorke. 1757
James Boone, ... 1758
John Potts, ... 1759
John Potts, ... 1760
John Potts, ... 1761
John Ross, ... 1762
John Ross, ... 1763
John Ross, ... 1764
Adam Witman, ... 1765
Adam Witman, ... 1766
Edward Biddle, ... 1767
Edward Biddle, ... 1768
Edward Biddle, ... 1769
Edward Biddle, ... 1770
Edward Biddle, ... 1771
Henry Christ, ... 1771
Edward Biddle, ... 1772
Henry Christ, ... 1772
Edward Biddle, ... 1773
Henry Christ, ... 1773
Edward Biddle, (Speaker,) 1774
Henry Christ, ... 1774
Edward Biddle, ... 1775
Henry Christ, ... 1775
Henry Haller, (additional,) 1776
John Lesher, (additional,) 1776

OFFICERS FOR CUMBERLAND COUNTY.

Sheriffs.

John Potter,	Oct.	6, 1750
Ezekiel Dunning,	Oct.	3, 1751–53
John Potter,	Oct.	4, 1754–55
William Parker,	Oct.	5, 1756
Ezekiel Smith,	Oct.	4, 1759–60
Ezekiel Dunning,	Oct.	4, 1762
John Holmes,	Oct.	5, 1765–67
David Hoge,	Oct.	6, 1768–70
Ephraim Blaine,	Oct.	7, 1771–73
Robert Semple,	Oct.	6, 1774–75

Coroners.

Adam Hoops,	Oct.	6, 1750
Tobias Hendricks,	Oct.	3, 1751–52
John McClure,	Oct.	3, 1753–54
Ezekiel Dunning,	Oct.	4, 1755
John McClure,	Oct.	5, 1756
John Miller,	Oct.	4, 1759
Robert Robb,	Oct.	3, 1760–62
Joseph Hunter,	Oct.	4, 1763
William McCoskry,	Oct.	9, 1764
James Jack,	Oct.	5, 1765–57
William Denney,	Oct.	6, 1768–70
Samuel Laird,	Oct.	7, 1771–73
James Pollock,	Oct.	6, 1774–75

Deputy Surveyor.

John Armstrong,	Oct.	9, 1753

Collectors.

James Lindsay,	1751–56
Nathaniel Wilson, (resigned,)	1757
Benjamin Chambers,	1758
William Brown,	1761–62
John Lindsay,	1763
James Lindsay,	1764–69
John Holmes, appointed 1770, (not accepted.)	
Thomas Baird,	1770–74
Thomas Baird, Jr.,	1775–76

CUMBERLAND COUNTY.

Treasurers.

John Calhoun,	1757
John Byers,	1758–59
Robert Miller,	1761
William Miller,	1762–65
William Brown,	1766
John Montgomery,	1767–76

Prothonotary, Clerk of Courts, Register and Recorder.

Turbutt Francis,	May	21, 1770
Hermanus Alricks.		

Justices of the Peace.

Samuel Smith,	March	10, 1749
William Maxwell,	March	10, 1749
George Croghan,	March	10, 1749
Robert Dunning,	March	10, 1749
Matthew Dill,	March	10, 1769
Benjamin Chambers,	March	10, 1749
William Trent,	March	10, 1749
William Allison,	March	10, 1749
Hermanus Alricks,	March	10, 1749
John Miller,	March	10, 1749
Robert Chambers,	March	10, 1749
John Finley,	March	10, 1749
Thomas Wilson,	March	10, 1749
Samuel Smith,		1750
William Maxwell,		1750
George Croghan,		1750
Benjamin Chambers,		1750
Robert Chambers,		1750
William Allison,		1750
William Trent,		1750
John Finley,		1750
John Miller,		1750
Hermanus Alricks,		1750
James Galbraith,		1750
James Hamilton,	July	13, 1757
Benjamin Shoemaker,	July	13, 1757
Members of Proprietary and Governor's Council,	July	13, 1757
Francis West,	July	13, 1757
John Smith,	July	13, 1757
William Smith,	July	13, 1757
David Wilson,	July	13, 1757
John Armstrong,	July	13, 1757
John Potter,	July	13, 1757

John McKnight,	July	13, 1757
James Caruthers,	July	13, 1757
Joseph Armstrong,	July	13, 1757
Hugh Mercer,	July	13, 1757
John Byers,	July	13, 1757
Hermanus Alricks,	July	13, 1757
Members of Proprietary and Governor's Council,	Oct.	17, 1764
John Armstrong,	Oct.	17, 1764
James Galbraith,	Oct.	17, 1764
John Byers,	Oct.	17, 1764
William Smith,	Oct.	17, 1764
John McKnight,	Oct.	17, 1764
James Caruthers,	Oct.	17, 1764
Hermanus Alricks,	Oct.	17, 1764
Adam Hoops,	Oct.	17, 1764
Francis Campbell,	Oct.	17, 1764
John Reynolds,	Oct.	17, 1764
Jonathan Hoge,	Oct.	17, 1764
Robert Miller,	Oct.	17, 1764
William Lyon,	Oct.	17, 1764
Robert Callender,	Oct.	17, 1764
Andrew Calhoun,	Oct.	17, 1764
James Maxwell,	Oct.	17, 1764
Samuel Perry,	Oct.	17, 1764
John Holmes,	Oct.	17, 1764
John Allison,	Oct.	17, 1764
James Elliot,	May	9, 1767
Bernard Dougherty,	May	9, 1767
George Robinson,	May	9, 1767
William Patterson,	Feb.	19, 1768
Turbutt Francis,	May	21, 1770
Members of Council,	May	23, 1770
John Armstrong,	May	23, 1770
James Galbraith,	May	23, 1770
John Byers,	May	23, 1770
James Caruthers,	May	23, 1770
Hermanus Alricks,	May	23, 1770
John Reynolds,	May	23, 1770
Jonathan Hoge,	May	23, 1770
Robert Miller,	May	23, 1770
William Lyon,	May	23, 1770
Robert Callender,	May	23, 1770
Andrew Calhoun,	May	23, 1770
James Maxwell,	May	23, 1770
Samuel Perry,	May	23, 1770
John Holmes,	May	23, 1770

John Allison,	May	23, 1770
Christopher Lemes,	May	23, 1770
Bernard Dougherty,	May	23, 1770
George Robinson,	May	23, 1770
William Patterson,	May	23, 1770
Turbutt Francis,	May	23, 1770
William Maclay,	May	23, 1770
Arthur St. Clair,	May	23, 1770
Henry Prather,	May	23, 1770
William Crawford,	May	23, 1770
James Milligan,	May	23, 1770
Thomas Gist,	May	23, 1770
Dorsey Pentecost,	May	23, 1770
John Agnew,	May	23, 1770
John Armstrong,	April	6, 1771
John Byers,	April	6, 1771
John Reynolds,	April	6, 1771
Jonathan Hoge,	April	6, 1771
Robert Miller,	April	6, 1771
William Lyon,	April	6, 1771
Turbutt Francis,	April	6, 1771
Henry Prather,	April	6, 1771
John Agnew,	April	6, 1771
William Thompson,	April	6, 1771
James Oliver,	April	6, 1771
Matthew Henderson,	April	6, 1771
Andrew Calhoun,	April	6, 1771
James Maxwell,	April	6, 1771
John Holmes,	April	6, 1771
John Allison,	April	6, 1771
George Robinson,	April	6, 1771
William Patterson,	April	6, 1771
John Maclay, Jr.,	April	6, 1771
William Elliott,	April	6, 1771
William Brown	April	6, 1771
Samuel Lyon,	April	6, 1771
James Dunlap,	April	6, 1771

Assembly.

Joseph Armstrong,	1750
Hermanus Alricks,	1750
Daniel Williams,	1751
William Trent,	1751
Joseph Armstrong,	1752
John Armstrong,	1752
Joseph Armstrong,	1753

John Armstrong, ...	1753
Joseph Armstrong, ...	1754
John Smith, ...	1754
Joseph Armstrong, ...	1755
John Smith, ...	1755
William West, ...	1756
William Allen, ...	1756
John Stanwix, ...	1757
William Allen, ...	1757
William Allen, ...	1758
John Smith, ...	1758
William Allen, ...	1759
John Smith, ...	1759
William Allen, ...	1760
John Byers, ...	1760
William Allen, ...	1761
John Byers, ...	1761
William Allen, ...	1762
James Galbraith, ...	1762
William Allen, ...	1763 to 1775
John Montgomery, ...	1763 to 1775
Jonathan Hoge, (additional,)	1776
Robert Whitehill, (additional,)	1776

OFFICERS FOR NORTHAMPTON COUNTY.

Sheriffs.

William Craig, ...	Oct.	4, 1752
Nicholas Scull, ...	Oct.	3, 1753–55
John Rinker, ...	Oct.	4, 1756
John Moore, ...	Oct.	4, 1759–60
John Jennings, ...	Oct.	5, 1761–63
Peter Kachlein, ...	Oct.	4, 1764–66
John Jennings, ...	Oct.	5, 1767–69
Peter Kachlein, ...	Oct.	4, 1770–72
Henry Fuller, (Vollert,)	Oct.	4, 1773
Henry Fuller, (Vollert,)	Oct.	5, 1774–75

Coroners.

Thomas Wilson, ...	Oct.	4, 1752
Jasper Scull, ...	Oct.	3, 1753–54
Thomas Armstrong, ...	Oct.	4, 1755–56
John VanEtten, ...	Oct.	4, 1759

John VanEtten,	Oct.	3, 1760
Arthur Lattimore,	Oct.	4, 1762–63
David Berhinger,	Oct.	4, 1764–67
Robert Lattimore,	Oct.	6, 1768
William Ledlie,	Oct.	5, 1769–70
Peter Seip,	Oct.	5, 1771–72
Samuel Rea,	Oct.	4, 1773
Jonas Hartzell,	Oct.	6, 1775

Collectors.

Daniel Craig,	1753–6
John Jones,	1757–66
Jesse Jones,	1767–76

Treasurers.

Nicholas Scull, Jr.,	1757–9
John Wagle,	1759
Adam Yohe,	1762–4
John Wagle,	1765–72
Herman Schnyder,	1773–6
John Mush,	1776

Prothonotary and Clerk of Orphans' Court.

Lewis Gordon,	Dec.	13, 1759

Justices of the Peace.

Thomas Craig,	June	9, 1752
Daniel Brodhead,	June	9, 1752
Timothy Horsfield,	June	9, 1752
Hugh Wilson,	June	9, 1752
James Martin,	June	9, 1752
John Van Etten,	June	9, 1752
Aaron Dupui,	June	9, 1752
William Craig,	June	9, 1752
William Parsons,	June	9, 1752
William Parsons,	Sept.	4, 1758
William Plumsted,	Nov.	27, 1757
Thomas Craig,	Nov.	27, 1757
Hugh Wilson,	Nov.	27, 1757
James Martin,	Nov.	27, 1757
Timothy Horsfield,	Nov.	27, 1757
Peter Trexler,	Nov.	27, 1757
Aaron Dupui,	Nov.	27, 1757
William Parsons,	Nov.	27, 1757
Lewis Klotz,	Nov.	27, 1757

George Rex,	Nov.	27, 1757
Thomas Armstrong,	Nov.	27, 1757
Conrad Hess,	Nov.	27, 1757
The Members of Council,	Nov.	19, 1764
William Plumsted,	Nov.	19, 1764
Thomas Craig,	Nov.	19, 1764
Hugh Wilson,	Nov.	19, 1764
Aaron Dupui,	Nov.	19, 1764
Lewis Klotz,	Nov.	19, 1764
Thomas Armstrong,	Nov.	19, 1764
George Taylor,	Nov.	19, 1764
Lewis Gordon,	Nov.	19, 1764
Jacob Arndt,	Nov.	19, 1764
John Moore,	Nov.	19, 1764
Robert Lyle,	Nov.	19, 1764
James Allen,	Nov.	19, 1764
John Jennings,	Nov.	19, 1764
Henry Geiger,	Nov.	19, 1764
Daniel Brodhead,	Nov.	19, 1764
The Members of Council,	March	15, 1766
George Taylor,	March	15, 1766
Thomas Craig,	March	15, 1766
Hugh Wilson,	March	15, 1766
Aaron Dupui,	March	15, 1766
Lewis Klotz,	March	15, 1766
Thomas Armstrong,	March	15, 1766
Lewis Gordon,	March	15, 1766
Jacob Arndt,	March	15, 1766
John Moore,	March	15, 1766
James Allen,	March	15, 1766
John Jennings,	March	15, 1766
Daniel Brodhead,	March	15, 1766
Robert Levers,	March	15, 1766
Christopher Waggoner,	March	15, 1766
Henry Kooken,	March	15, 1766
Joseph Gaston,	March	15, 1766
Garret Brodhead,	March	3, 1770
John Van Campen,	March	3, 1770
Lewis Klotz,		1773
Henry Kooken,		1773
Charles Stewart,		1773
Amos Ogden,		1773
Members of Council,	March	9, 1774
George Taylor, (Ded. Pot.,)	March	9, 1774
Aaron Dupui,	March	9, 1774
Lewis Klotz,	March	9, 1774

Lewis Gordon, (Ded. Pot.,)	March	9, 1774
Jacob Arndt,	March	9, 1774
James Allen,	March	9, 1774
John Jennings,	March	9, 1774
Robert Levers,	March	9, 1774
Christopher Waggoner,	March	9, 1774
Henry Kooken,	March	9, 1774
Joseph Gaston,	March	9, 1774
Garret Brodhead,	March	9, 1774
John Van Campen,	March	9, 1774
Lewis Nicola,	March	9, 1774
Arthur Lattimore,	March	9, 1774
Peter Kachlein,	March	9, 1774
John Wetzel,	March	9, 1774
Simon Dreisbach,	March	9, 1774
Jacob Lesh,	March	9, 1774
John Okely,	March	9, 1774
Nicholas Dupui,	March	9, 1774
Jacob Morrey,	March	9, 1774
Peter Trexler,	March	9, 1774
Samuel Rea,	March	9, 1774
Felix Lynn,	March	9, 1774

Assembly.

James Burnside,	1752
Willlam Parsons,	1753
James Burnside,	1754
William Edmonds,	1755
William Allen, (did not serve—chose to represent Cumberland,)	1756
William Plumsted,	1757
Lodowick Beeting,	1758
Lodowick Beeting,	1759
Lodowick Beeting,	1760
John Moore,	1761
John Moore,	1762
John Tool,	1763
George Taylor,	1764
George Taylor,	1765
George Taylor,	1766
George Taylor,	1767
George Taylor,	1768
George Taylor,	1769
William Edmonds,	1770
William Edmonds,	1771
William Edmonds,	1772
William Edmonds,	1773

197

William Edmonds,	1774
Peter Kachlein,	1775
George Taylor,	1776
James Allen, (additional,)	1776
Jacob Arndt, (additional,)	1776

OFFICERS FOR BEDFORD COUNTY.

Sheriffs.

John Proctor,	Oct.	8, 1771–2
James Piper,	Oct.	9, 1773–5

Coroners.

Joseph Erwin,	Oct.	8, 1771–2
John Cesna,	Oct.	9, 1773–4
John Stillwell,	Oct.	12, 1775

Collectors.

Thomas Urie,	1771–5
Robert Moore,	1775–6

Treasurer.

George Woods,	1773–4

Prothonotary, Register, and Recorder.

Arthur St. Clair,	March	12, 1771
Thomas Smith,	Feb.	27, 1773

Justices of the Peace.

John Frazer, (Dedimus Potestatem,)	March	11, 1771
Bernard Dougherty, (Dedimus Potestatem,)	March	11, 1771
Arthur St. Clair, (Dedimus Potestatem,)	March	11, 1771
William Crawford,	March	11, 1771
James Milligan,	March	11, 1771
Thomas Gist,	March	11, 1771
Dorsey Pentecost,	March	11, 1771
Alexander McKee,	March	11, 1771
William Proctor, Jr.,	March	11, 1771
John Hanna,	March	11, 1771
William Lochry,	March	11, 1771
John Willson,	March	11, 1771
Robert Cluggage,	March	11, 1771
William McConnell,	March	11, 1771

George Woods,	March	11, 1771
Abraham Keble,	Nov.	23, 1771
Arthur St. Clair, (special commission,)	Nov.	23, 1771
John Frazer, (Dedimus Potestatem,)	Feb.	27, 1773
Bernard Dougherty, (Dedimus Potestatem,)	Feb.	27, 1773
Arthur St. Clair,	Feb.	27, 1773
William Proctor, Jr.,	Feb.	27, 1773
Robert Cluggage,	Feb.	27, 1773
William McConnell,	Feb.	27, 1773
George Woods,	Feb.	27, 1773
Abraham Keble,	Feb.	27, 1773
Thomas Smith, (Dedimus Potestatem,)	Feb.	27, 1773
Thomas Coulter,	Feb.	27, 1773
John Piper,	Feb.	27, 1773
Elias Stillwell,	Feb.	27, 1773
Abraham Miley,	Feb.	27, 1773
Richard Hogeland,	Feb.	27, 1773
Bernard Dougherty, (Dedimus Potestatem,)	April	9, 1774
Arthur St. Clair,	April	9, 1774
William Proctor, Jr.,	April	9, 1774
Robert Cluggage,	April	9, 1774
George Woods,	April	9, 1774
Abraham Keble,	April	9, 1774
Thomas Smith, (Dedimus Potestatem,)	April	9, 1774
Thomas Coulter,	April	9, 1774
John Piper,	April	9, 1774
Elias Stillwell,	April	9, 1774
Abraham Miley,	April	9, 1774
Richard Hogeland,	April	9, 1774
Samuel Davidson,	April	9, 1774
Henry Lloyd,	April	9, 1774
William Latta,	April	9, 1774

Assembly.

William Thompson,	1771
William Thompson,	1772
George Woods,	1773
Bernard Dougherty,	1774
Bernard Dougherty,	1775
Thomas Smith, (additional,)	1776

Collector of Excise.

Thomas Urie,	1774

Clerk of Quarter Sessions of the Peace.

Arthur St. Clair,	Nov.	8, 1771

199

OFFICERS FOR NORTHUMBERLAND COUNTY.

Sheriffs.

William Cook, ...	Oct. 9, 1772–4
William Scull, ...	Oct. 12, 1775–6

Coroners.

James Parr, ...	Oct. 9, 1772
James Murray, ...	Oct. 9, 1773–4
Samuel Harris, ...	Oct. 12, 1775–6

Prothonotary, Register, Recorder.

William Maclay, (three commissions,) . .	March 24, 1772

Clerk of the Peace and Quarter Sessions of the Peace.

William Maclay, ...	May 19, 1772

Collectors.

Thomas Lemon, ...	1772–4
James Kincaid, ...	1774–5
Alexander Hunter, ...	1775–6

Treasurer.

Alexander Hunter, ...	1773–5

Justices of the Peace.

William Plunket, ...	March 24, 1772
Turbutt Francis, ...	March 24, 1772
Samuel Hunter, ...	March 24, 1772
James Potter, ...	March 24, 1772
William Maclay, ...	March 24, 1772
Caleb Graydon, ...	March 24, 1772
Benjamin Allison, ...	March 24, 1772
Robert Moody, ...	March 24, 1772
John Lowdon, ...	March 24, 1772
Thomas Lemon, ...	March 24, 1772
Ellis Hughes, ...	March 24, 1772
Benjamin Weiser, ...	March 24, 1772
William Patterson, ...	1773
Michael Troy, ...	1773
John Fleming, ...	1773
Samuel Maclay, ...	July 29, 1775
John Simpson, ...	July 29, 1775
Robert Robb, ...	July 29, 1775

WESTMORELAND COUNTY.

Evan Owen,	July	29, 1775
John Weitzel,	July	29, 1775
Henry Antes,	July	29, 1775

Assembly.

Samuel Hunter,	1772
Samuel Hunter,	1773
Samuel Hunter,	1774
Samuel Hunter,	1775
James Potter, (additional,)	1776

OFFICERS FOR WESTMORELAND COUNTY.

Sheriffs.

John Proctor,	Oct.	19, 1773
John Carnahan,	Oct.	13, 1774–75

Coronors.

James Kincaid,	Oct.	19, 1773–74
Francis Waddell,	Oct.	28, 1775

Prothonotary, Register, Recorder.

Arthur St. Clair,	Feb.	27, 1773
Michael Hoffnagle,	Mar.	26, 1776

Collector.

James Kincaid,	1773–74

Justices of the Peace.

William Crawford, (Ded. Pot.,)	Feb.	27, 1773
Arthur St. Clair, (Ded. Pot.,)	Feb.	27, 1773
Thomas Gist,	Feb.	27, 1773
Alexander McKee,	Feb.	27, 1773
Robert Hanna, (Ded. Pot.,)	Feb.	27, 1773
William Lochry,	Feb.	27, 1773
George Wilson,	Feb.	27, 1773
William Thompson,	Feb.	27, 1773
Æneas McKay,	Feb.	27, 1773
Joseph Spear,	Feb.	27, 1773
Alexander McClean,	Feb.	27, 1773
James Cavet,	Feb.	27, 1773
William Bracken,	Feb.	27, 1773
James Pollock,	Feb.	27, 1773

Samuel Sloan, ...	Feb.	27, 1773
Michael Rugh, ...	Feb.	27, 1773
Members of Council, ...	Jan.	11, 1774
William Crawford, (Ded. Pot.,) . . .	Jan.	11, 1774
Arthur St. Clair, (Ded. Pot.,)	Jan.	11, 1774
Thomas Gist, ...	Jan.	11, 1774
Alexander McKee, ...	Jan.	11, 1774
Robert Hanna, (Ded. Pot.,)	Jan.	11, 1774
William Lochry, ...	Jan.	11, 1774
William Bracken, ...	Jan.	11, 1774
James Pollock, ...	Jan.	11, 1774
Samuel Sloan, ...	Jan.	11, 1774
Michael Rugh, ...	Jan.	11, 1774
Van Swearingen, ...	Jan.	11, 1774
Thomas Scott, ...	Jan.	11, 1774
George Wilson, ...	Jan.	11, 1774
William Thompson, ...	Jan.	11, 1774
Æneas McKay, ...	Jan.	11, 1774
Joseph Spear, ...	Jan.	11, 1774
Alexander McClean, ...	Jan.	11, 1774
James Cavet, ...	Jan.	11, 1774
Alexander Ross, ...	Jan.	11, 1774
John Carnahan, ...	Jan.	11, 1774
Andrew McFarlane, ...	Jan.	11, 1774
Oliver Miller, ...	Jan.	11, 1774
Devereux Smith, ...	Jan.	11, 1774
John Shepherd, ...	Jan.	11, 1774

Assembly.

William Thompson, ...	1773
William Thompson, ...	1774
William Thompson, ...	1775
John Proctor, (additional,)	1776

INDEX

Richard, 26, 150,
154, 155, 156
House, George, 134
Houseman, John, 59
Houston, Alexander
Brown, 150
William, 55
Howard, Joseph, 172
Howell, Jacob, 95
Joshua, 112, 135,
138
Samuel, 136, 143
William, 26, 78
Hubley, Bernard, 176
Hudde, Andreas, 9,
10
Hudson, Samuel, 121
William, 131,
132, 137, 140
Hugh, Michael, 202
Hughes, Ellis, 200
John, 112, 127,
128, 186
Mathew, 148
Matthew, 149, 150
William, 91, 92,
93, 151, 159,
160, 161, 162
Hulings, Michael,
138
Humphreys, Charles,
76, 97, 98, 99
David, 109
James, 37, 38,
100, 111, 112,
113, 115, 139
William, 113,
114, 135
Hunt, Roger, 83, 94,
95, 96
Hunter, Alexander,
200
James, 83
John, 56
Joseph, 190
Samuel, 200, 201
Hussey, John, 55
Huston, Alexander,
135
Hutton, Joseph, 183
Hyatt, John, 99, 138
Huygen, Hendrick, 9
Ingels, Richard, 36
Ingersoll, Jared, 35
Ingham, Jonathan,
151, 152, 153,
164, 165
Inglis, John, 134
Ingram, Job, 69
Irish, Nathaniel,
150
Irons, Simon, 57,
58, 61, 62, 63
Thomas, 59, 60

Irwin, Samuel, 115
Jack, James, 190
Jackson, Ephraim, 87
Joseph, 144
Richard, 37
Samuel, 186
Jacquet, John Paul,
10, 15, 16
Jacobs, Albertus, 70
Alfred, 66
Bartholomew, 159
Israel, 129, 130
John, 64
John, 67, 68, 96,
97, 98, 99
James, Abel, 138,
143
Henry, 16
James, 51, 68,
80, 91
Joseph, 94, 95
Mordecai, 82
Thomas, 51, 52,
53, 100
Jameson, David, 183,
184
Jamison, David, 36,
185
John, 150, 151,
152
Janney, Abel, 76,
146, 147, 157,
159
Thomas, 26, 145,
146, 150. 151
Jansen, Derrick,
106, 107, 108,
109
Harman, 12
January, Thomas, 51
Jarey, Isaac, 13
Jenkins, Jabez, 56
William, 78, 85
Jenks, Thomas, 168
Jenney, Robert, 35
Jennings, Edward,
56
John, 194, 196,
197
Samuel, 28
Jestis, Jestell, 120
Jevon, William, 175
Jewell, Robert, 100
Job, Andrew, 75, 76,
79, 86
Johnson, Benjamin,
57
Claus, 18, 145
Johnston, Alexander,
82, 83, 84
Samuel, 182, 183,
184
Jolly, Charles, 114,
115

Jones, Benjamin,
148, 149, 150,
159, 160, 161,
162
Daniel, 57, 58,
61, 62
David, 173, 174
Edward, 119
Evan, 58, 59, 145
Griffith, 26, 32,
63, 116, 118,
119, 130, 136
Isaac, 112, 113,
114, 115, 132,
138
Jesse, 195
John, 48, 52, 53,
103, 111, 112,
123, 136, 137,
195
Owen, 31
Robert, 104, 104,
105, 106, 118,
119, 120, 121,
123, 124, 125
Samuel, 172, 173
Thomas, 119
Jonsten, Jaes, 12
Joyce, John, 101
Kachlein, Peter,
194, 197, 198
Karnaghan, John, 80
Kearsley, John, 141,
142
Keble, Abraham, 199
Keen, Matthias, 119,
153
Keift, Sir William,
9
Keith, Alexander, 48
Sir William, 24,
33, 122
Kelly, Edward, 40
Kennerly, James, 75
Kepple, Henry, 128
Kerlin, John, 76
Kern, Jacob, 186
Key, Joseph, 89
Moses, 90
Keyser, Derrick,
109, 110
Kidd, John, 152, 153
Killen, Robert, 60
Kincaid, James, 200
201
King, John, 14, 130
138
Walter, 116
William, 181
Kinsey, John, 31,
32, 33, 39,
122, 123, 124,
125, 126
Kipp, Hendrick, 12

216

218

www.ingramcontent.com/pod-product-compliance
Lightning Source LLC
Chambersburg PA
CBHW070417270326
41926CB00014B/2830